U.S. Strategy for
Pakistan and Afghanistan

COUNCIL *on*
FOREIGN
RELATIONS

Independent Task Force Report No. 65

Richard L. Armitage and
Samuel R. Berger, *Chairs*
Daniel S. Markey, *Project Director*

U.S. Strategy for Pakistan and Afghanistan

© **Mixed Sources**
Product group from well-managed forests, controlled sources and recycled wood or fiber
www.fsc.org Cert no. SW-COC-001530
© 1996 Forest Stewardship Council
FSC

Task Force Members

Task Force members are asked to join a consensus signifying that they endorse "the general policy thrust and judgments reached by the group, though not necessarily every finding and recommendation." They participate in the Task Force in their individual, not institutional, capacities.

Richard L. Armitage
Armitage International L.C.

Reza Aslan
University of California, Riverside

J. Brian Atwood
University of Minnesota

David W. Barno
Center for a New American Security

Samuel R. Berger
Albright Stonebridge Group

Karan K. Bhatia
General Electric Company

Marshall M. Bouton
Chicago Council on Global Affairs

Steve Coll
New America Foundation

Joseph J. Collins
National War College

James F. Dobbins
RAND Corporation

C. Christine Fair
Georgetown University

John A. Gastright
DynCorp International

Robert L. Grenier
ERG Partners

John M. Keane
SCP Partners

Michael Krepon
Henry L. Stimson Center

Sloan C. Mann
Development Transformations

Daniel S. Markey
Council on Foreign Relations

John A. Nagl
Center for a New American Security

John D. Negroponte
McLarty Associates

Charles S. Robb
George Mason University

Contents

Foreword

It is now nine years since the United States first went to war in Afghanistan. The rationale for doing so in the aftermath of the 9/11 attacks was clear. Now, however, the United States has embarked on a different and considerably more ambitious undertaking in Afghanistan that affects—and is affected by—the complex political currents of Pakistan and its border regions. It is not clear that U.S. interests warrant such an investment. Nor is it clear that the effort will succeed.

In Pakistan, a weak civilian government is struggling to cope with a plethora of challenges exacerbated by this summer's floods. The military has lost more than two thousand men in an ongoing battle with insurgents in the country's northwest. But the army does not fight all militants equally. Islamabad's ongoing tolerance of—and even support for—extremist groups that target American interests in Afghanistan and globally calls into question the basis of the U.S. relationship with Pakistan.

In Afghanistan, the Taliban insurgency is more violent than at any point since the U.S. invasion after 9/11. NATO forces are paying a heavy toll. Afghan public enthusiasm for the government is waning after years of unmet expectations. The economy, devastated by more than thirty years of war, has not recovered sufficiently to provide for the people, while the government remains largely ineffective and riven by corruption.

The Obama administration, about to embark on its third policy review in two years, must decide how best to address these challenges, given local realities, growing U.S. debt, and wide public skepticism about the present U.S. strategy.

This Council on Foreign Relations–sponsored Independent Task Force sought to identify U.S. interests and objectives in Pakistan and Afghanistan, assess existing policy, explore the potential of alternative strategies, and make recommendations for future policy. The Task Force offers a qualified endorsement of President Obama's approach to the region, including the expansion of U.S. assistance to Pakistan, the surge of military forces in Afghanistan to roughly one hundred thousand, and the commitment to begin drawing down those forces in July 2011.

Yet the Task Force also highlights a number of potential problems with the policy, emphasizing Pakistan's tolerance of and support for dangerous terrorist groups, weak state institutions, contentious relations with India, and nuclear weapons. The Task Force recommends easing U.S. trade restrictions on Pakistani textile exports, assisting a rapid recovery from the floods, deepening an ongoing dialogue on nuclear issues, and increasing the military's capacity to defeat militants on the battlefield. At the same time, the Task Force argues that Washington should act against terrorists operating from Pakistani soil, including al-Qaeda and Lashkar-e-Taiba, and the United States should leave no uncertainty in Islamabad that a sustainable partnership will depend on a Pakistani break with all terrorist groups.

In Afghanistan, the Task Force notes that the Obama administration will need to find a way to address the government's weakness, corruption, and political division; determine the terms of reference for negotiations with the Taliban; increase the quantity and, even more, the quality of Afghan security forces; and encourage the development of Afghanistan's economy while decreasing the production of drugs. If the December 2010 review of U.S. strategy in Afghanistan concludes that the present strategy is not working, the Task Force recommends that a shift to a more limited mission at a substantially reduced level of military force would be warranted.

I would like to thank the Task Force's chairs, Richard Armitage and Samuel Berger, whose leadership, expertise, and diplomacy were integral to the success of this effort. I would also like to thank the Task Force members, an extraordinary group of people who committed a great deal of time, talent, and thought to this endeavor. My thanks go as well to Anya Schmemann, director of CFR's Task Force Program, for her efforts in guiding this project from beginning to end. Daniel Markey, senior fellow for India, Pakistan, and South Asia, also has my thanks for directing this project and writing the final report. All have contributed to a timely, richly detailed, and substantive report that will help clarify the stakes and the options for the United States in South Asia.

Richard N. Haass
President
Council on Foreign Relations
November 2010

Acknowledgments

This report on U.S. strategy for Pakistan and Afghanistan is the product of the Independent Task Force, and I am deeply appreciative of the members' and observers' expertise and guidance. Our distinguished chairs, Sandy Berger and Richard Armitage, were active and dynamic leaders, and I am indebted to them for the time and attention they devoted to this project in all of its facets. We are also grateful to Senator Chuck Hagel, who helped to guide the project during its early stages.

In February 2010, the chairs and I were graciously hosted by Ambassador Anne Patterson in Pakistan and Ambassador Karl Eikenberry and General Stanley McChrystal in Afghanistan. We benefited from informative U.S. and NATO briefings in Islamabad, Kabul, and Kandahar. During that trip, we met with numerous senior Pakistani and Afghan civilian and military officials as well as independent scholars, politicians, business leaders, and journalists.

I also had the opportunity to travel to the region in October 2009 to conduct preliminary research for this report. That trip would not have been possible if not for assistance provided by the U.S. Department of State, our able ambassadors in Islamabad and Kabul, and their hard-working teams. A special thanks goes to the International Security Assistance Force (ISAF) Strategic Advisory Group for facilitating meetings and travel in Afghanistan.

We are thankful to Admiral Michael Mullen, Ambassador Richard Holbrooke, and their capable staff members, who briefed the members of the Task Force. I am also thankful to a great many U.S. officials in Washington, DC, as well as diplomats posted in the Pakistani and Afghan embassies, who met with me to discuss the challenges of the region.

We received helpful input from many CFR members, including at roundtables in Washington, DC, led by Task Force member Steve Coll, and in New York, led by Task Force member Lieutenant General David Barno.

I am grateful to many at CFR: CFR's Publications team assisted in editing the report and readied it for publication, and CFR's Communications, Meetings, Corporate, External Affairs, and Outreach teams all worked to ensure that the report reaches the widest audience possible.

Anya Schmemann and Kristin Lewis of CFR's Task Force Program were instrumental to this project from beginning to end. Their wisdom, experience, and good sense kept this challenging project on track. I would also like to thank my three research associates—Daniel Simons, Robert Nelson, and Kunaal Sharma—who each provided invaluable assistance in ways both large and small. This final product owes a great debt to their energy, time, and abundant intellectual talents.

I am grateful to CFR President Richard N. Haass for giving me the opportunity to direct this effort. This project was made possible by the generous support of the Rockefeller Foundation and by David M. Rubenstein's support for the Task Force Program. CFR also expresses its thanks to the Starr Foundation for its support of the Asia studies program.

Daniel S. Markey
Project Director

Task Force Report

Introduction

Al-Qaeda's attack on September 11, 2001, was the deadliest terrorist assault on the United States in history. In the hours and days that followed, Americans learned more about the perpetrators and their links to bases and networks in Afghanistan and Pakistan. Less than a month later, President George W. Bush launched Operation Enduring Freedom. Much changed nearly overnight as the United States focused military, economic, and diplomatic attention squarely on the region for the first time since the end of the Cold War. In Afghanistan, the Taliban regime—al-Qaeda's sympathetic host—was toppled. In Pakistan, the Pervez Musharraf regime was drafted into Washington's Global War on Terror.

Too quickly, however, the war in Iraq diverted U.S. attention and resources. Over subsequent years the Taliban regrouped, top al-Qaeda leaders managed to elude justice, and terrorist violence in Pakistan and Afghanistan spiked. Now, nine years into the Afghan war, many Americans and U.S. allies have grown weary of conflict, unsure about U.S. objectives, and uncertain about U.S. prospects for success.

The Task Force shares these concerns. Americans have already paid dearly: more than one thousand U.S. men and women serving in Afghanistan or Pakistan have lost their lives, and thousands more have suffered injuries and wounds and are trying to recover. Hopes for an immediate turnaround in southern Afghanistan have not been realized. The underlying dynamics in Afghanistan remain stubborn—pervasive corruption that breeds the insurgency; weak governance that creates a vacuum; Taliban resilience that feeds an atmosphere of intimidation; and an erratic leader whose agenda may not be the same as that of the United States. In Pakistan, devastating floods are placing enormous new stresses on the state—already challenged by political, economic, and security problems—increasing disaffection among its people, and weakening its ability to fight extremists in its territory.

3

The outcomes of these struggles are still uncertain. But the stakes are high. What happens in Afghanistan and Pakistan matters to Americans.

Americans will be less safe if a network of like-minded terrorist groups, including al-Qaeda, can operate freely in large portions of Afghanistan and Pakistan. These groups have repeatedly demonstrated their willingness and ability to conduct deadly attacks on the United States, India, and U.S. allies. Their anti-American fervor is undiminished.

Americans will be less secure if turmoil—possibly even civil war—in Afghanistan threatens the stability of Pakistan and the region, thus increasing tensions between Pakistan and India. Significant unrest in Afghanistan could produce a proxy war, as regional powers seek to secure their interests.

Americans will also be at greater risk if extremists in Pakistan exploit the country's devastating floods, fragile institutions, and internal conflict to undermine the Pakistani state. These risks are compounded by Pakistan's nuclear arsenal and the potential for nuclear material to fall into dangerous hands.

A strategy for addressing these threats has been put in place by the United States and the North Atlantic Treaty Organization (NATO) over the past eighteen months. That strategy seeks to weaken the Taliban sufficiently to allow the Afghan people to safely reject it; develop Afghan security forces so that Afghans can defend themselves as U.S. troops leave; and, through an enhanced civilian effort, help the Afghan government sustain the support of its people by providing basic services. Taliban fighters are more likely to lay down arms if they are under pressure, and a weakened Taliban is more likely to negotiate on acceptable terms—outcomes the United States should encourage. Reconciliation with senior Taliban leaders on appropriate terms must be part of the United States' overall strategy. Irregular conflicts rarely end in a surrender ceremony on a battleship.

The surge of forces—military and civilian—to carry out that strategy was completed in August 2010. There are some hopeful signs of progress, such as the training of the Afghan security forces and the targeting of Taliban networks. But in other areas the trends are less encouraging.

The cloudy picture and high costs raise the question of whether the United States should now downsize its ambitions and reduce its military presence in Afghanistan. Such a shift is not without its own significant risks. U.S. forces would operate in a deteriorating security environment. Drawing down troops could make it harder to move around the country to collect intelligence and attack the enemy; complicate the training of the Afghan National Security Forces (ANSF), which are greatly enhanced by partnering with NATO forces; increase the potential for the Taliban to consolidate its control of significant portions of Afghanistan; and provoke regional and ethnic conflicts.

That said, the current U.S. approach is at a critical point. President Barack Obama will undertake a review in December 2010 with a view toward beginning to draw down the surge in July 2011. That review should involve more than an evaluation of which provinces and districts now warrant an Afghan security lead. It should mark the start of a clear-eyed assessment of whether there is sufficient overall progress to conclude that the strategy is working. It should address some fundamental questions, including: Has there been a significant improvement in the capabilities of the ANSF? Is momentum shifting against the insurgency in contested areas? Once NATO operations have taken place, is normal life starting to return? Is progress being made in building local security and civilian capabilities? Has the government in Kabul taken serious steps to combat corruption?

This review should continue into 2011 if additional time is needed to make a thorough assessment. The president has said that the United States will continue its present military surge until July 2011. If there is confidence that the current strategy is working, then that should enable the United States to steadily draw down its forces starting in July, based on conditions on the ground, as the president has announced. If not, however, a more significant drawdown to a narrower military mission would be warranted. The United States also cannot justify its current level of effort if it does not have the full support of the Afghan government. Washington should pursue a political strategy that continues to press Afghan president Hamid Karzai for needed reforms, including on anticorruption issues, but at the same time seeks to amplify the voices of Afghanistan's local and provincial leaders, political parties, and the parliament.

The Obama administration's strategy in Pakistan has resulted in stronger relationships with civilian and military authorities, more substantial and targeted aid, and an unrelenting assault by unmanned aerial drones on the militant networks operating in the Federally Administered Tribal Areas (FATA). The U.S. commitment to a long-term strategic partnership with Pakistan is a critical step in securing Pakistani action against the militant groups within its borders. The tragic floods in August have the potential either to demonstrate U.S. commitment to the long-term well-being of the Pakistani people or to undo much of the work that the United States has done. A continuing robust response is necessary to prevent Pakistan from sliding into economic and political collapse.

We write this report respectful of the sacrifice Americans are already making in Afghanistan. We respect the president's commitment to the war effort and the decisions he has made to protect U.S. national security. We are mindful of the real threat we face. But we are also aware of the costs of the present strategy. We cannot accept these costs unless the strategy begins to show signs of progress.

THE THREAT

Militants in Pakistan and Afghanistan pose a direct threat to the United States and its allies. They jeopardize the stability of Pakistan, a nuclear power that lives in an uneasy peace with its rival, India.

U.S.- and NATO-led military operations have cleared the vast majority of international terrorist training camps in Afghanistan. But top al-Qaeda leaders and other international terrorists fled to Pakistan, where they continue to plan attacks against the United States and its allies. Since 9/11, there have been more than a dozen serious attempts—some successful, some thwarted—to attack the United States and American allies that were planned or supported by groups on the Afghanistan-Pakistan border. These include the Times Square bomber in 2010; the plot against the New York subway system in 2009; the plan to attack the Barcelona metro system in 2008; the effort to bomb airliners in flight over the Atlantic in 2006; the attack on the London subway system in 2005 in which 52 civilians died; the Madrid attack in 2004 in which 191 civilians died; the Bali bombings in 2002 that killed 202 civilians; and other plots known and unknown to the general public.

Military operations in Afghanistan and missile strikes on the Pakistani side of the border have placed intense pressure on al-Qaeda and other militants. But the United States cannot destroy the threat posed by al-Qaeda without weakening the other extremist groups in the region that offer it resources and safe haven, including the Afghan Taliban. Parts of the Afghan Taliban can be brought into the political fold in Afghanistan; they are not the same as al-Qaeda. But other elements of the Taliban have established deep ideological and operational ties with al-Qaeda. Some of these elements, including fighters in the Haqqani network and allied groups like Lashkar-e-Taiba (LeT), are already active inside Afghanistan, and their ambitions are not limited to Pakistan's tribal areas. The United States cannot afford to underestimate the threat that they would pose to U.S. security if they gained even more operating space within Afghanistan. Nor can the United States overlook the fact that the Taliban's harsh tactics made them terrorists within their own country. There is no reason to expect that these facts have changed. A Taliban consolidation would mean brutal outrages against Afghan citizens, particularly women.

While al-Qaeda's radicalism has gained a treacherous foothold elsewhere, including Yemen and Somalia, the border regions between Afghanistan and Pakistan remain a stronghold and the headquarters for al-Qaeda's senior leaders. Al-Qaeda and its affiliates have deep ties to this region that make it a particularly dangerous home base. Afghanistan itself also represents a rallying cry for jihadists internationally who believe they toppled the Soviet Union there.

A Taliban stronghold in Afghanistan that creates space for terrorists is not the only potentially dangerous scenario. Turmoil there—possibly even a bloody civil war—could produce a refugee crisis, draw in regional competitors, and destabilize Pakistan and the region. Increased militancy in Afghanistan could spill over into Pakistan, which already faces a dangerous insurgency as well as political and economic challenges.

The challenge of fighting regional terrorist networks is compounded by the fact that Pakistan draws distinctions between such groups. It acts aggressively against those that have taken up arms against the state, such as the Pakistani Taliban, while elements of its security services provide passive and active support to groups that target Afghanistan, India, and others. Afghan Taliban leaders have operated from inside Pakistan since they were toppled by the United States, and many of their leaders commute to the war in Afghanistan and draw war supplies from Pakistani sanctuaries.

The Haqqani network—an Afghan Taliban affiliate based inside Pakistan's FATA—is responsible for a range of attacks on U.S., Afghan, and Indian targets inside Afghanistan. Other militant organizations such as LeT, the group responsible for the deadly November 2008 attack on Mumbai, go virtually untouched by Pakistani authorities. Another terror event on the scale of that attack could provoke a disastrous crisis between India and Pakistan. LeT is also one of a number of terrorist groups recruiting U.S. citizens in an effort to extend its reach and avoid detection. Left unchecked, LeT and its affiliates could eventually surpass al-Qaeda as the world's most sophisticated and dangerous terrorist organization.

Despite the commitment of more than 140,000 Pakistani troops—and losing over two thousand soldiers—to push back the Pakistani Taliban, terrorists have continued to execute brazen attacks in Pakistan's largest cities.[1] The existence of extensive militant networks that target Pakistanis and their government is particularly dangerous given Pakistan's expanding nuclear program of between eighty and one hundred warheads. While Pakistan's military now exercises control of the nuclear arsenal, there are circumstances under which Pakistan's instability could result in nuclear material ending up in dangerous hands.

Terrorism and extremism in Pakistan feed on the other serious challenges it faces. The devastating floods of 2010, like the October 2005 earthquake, have demonstrated the tragic vulnerability of tens of millions of Pakistani citizens. Rapid population growth, diminishing natural resources, and poor economic prospects open the door to public alienation and internal violence. Pakistan's public and private institutions are not well prepared to meet these challenges without extensive outside assistance. Such times of need provide an opportunity for militant groups, many of which have charity arms, to take advantage of the power vacuum and to expand their networks. This latest tragedy could be overwhelming for a Pakistani government that is unable, even under normal circumstances, to provide for its people.

U.S. STRATEGIC OBJECTIVES

In Pakistan, the United States aims to degrade and defeat the terrorist groups that threaten American interests from its territory and to prevent turmoil that would imperil the Pakistani state and risk the security of Pakistan's nuclear program. These goals require a stable Pakistani partner. Even in the midst of the flood crisis and recovery, Washington should seek to encourage Pakistan to strengthen its efforts to unequivocally fight terrorism and extremism. Improving bilateral cooperation and contributing to Pakistan's economic, political, and military stability are all essential elements of this effort. Washington cannot, however, be the only one committed to partnership. To maintain momentum into the future, Pakistan must also show that it can generate stronger cooperation on issues of substantial interest to the United States.

In Afghanistan, the United States seeks to prevent the country from becoming a base for terrorist groups that target the United States and its allies and to diminish the potential that Afghanistan reverts to civil war, which would destabilize the region. After nine years of war, the United States must work to achieve these goals at a cost that will retain the continued support of the American public. That is best accomplished by enabling Afghans to shoulder a greater responsibility for their own security and working with other regional states to improve regional stability so that the U.S. troop presence can wind down. An acceptable end state in Afghanistan would be one in which the Afghan people are secure and strong enough to prevent the rise of new terrorist safe havens inside Afghanistan and avert a return to civil war without relying upon U.S. or international military forces.

CURRENT U.S. STRATEGY AND POLICY

In Pakistan, the United States has publicly committed to a long-term and consistent relationship with civilian and military leaders as the best means to achieve U.S. security objectives. In frequent senior-level dialogues, the Obama administration has sought to influence the strategic considerations of Pakistani leaders, convincing them that Pakistan is better off expanding its counterterror and counterinsurgency operations, strengthening the government's ability to serve its people, and improving the security of Pakistan's nuclear program. At the same time, Washington has expanded and intensified its use of drone strikes against terrorists based along the Afghan border, acting alone when Islamabad has been unwilling or unable to act.

Washington's efforts are aimed at shoring up Pakistani stability against the many threats it faces, from extremism and militancy to political and economic turmoil and the strain that large-scale flood relief and reconstruction is placing on the civilian government and the military. In recent years the U.S. Congress has authorized a tripling of nonmilitary assistance to Pakistan, up to $1.5 billion per year. Washington also provides reimbursements and military assistance to Pakistan, which, in FY 2010, totaled nearly $2 billion.[2]

In Afghanistan, the current U.S. strategy seeks to weaken Taliban insurgents in the field; provide security training and assistance for the Afghan people to defend themselves; and assist the Afghan government in providing basic services to deprive the insurgency of popular support and create conditions for sustainable security when NATO forces leave. President Obama has invested in a military surge with a corollary increase in civilian resources to give this strategy new momentum.

For the first time, U.S. forces have targeted the strongholds of the insurgency in southern Afghanistan with major operations, contesting areas where Taliban influence had gone virtually unchallenged for years. To degrade the Taliban, the United States has expanded conventional operations, greatly enhanced Special Forces activities targeting mid-grade Taliban leaders, and improved intelligence collection. The U.S. military has committed to strengthening the Afghan National Army (ANA) and Afghan National Police (ANP) as well as local community-based defense units through joint operations, training, equipping, mentoring, and partnering. By pressuring the Taliban, it has begun to set conditions for political settlements at the grassroots level by encouraging reintegration of Taliban fighters who give up the insurgency. At the senior levels, it has supported reconciliation with Taliban leaders if they meet necessary conditions.

On the civilian front, the United States is working with local and national Afghan officials to reduce corruption and make the government more responsive to the needs of the people. Washington has made a series of attempts to secure the full cooperation of President Karzai and his government. Other U.S. assistance, especially in the agricultural sector, has been devoted to enhancing economic opportunities so that Afghans have alternatives to insurgency and illicit activities, such as the narcotics trade.

CHALLENGES ON THE GROUND

President Obama inherited a difficult and deteriorating situation in Pakistan and Afghanistan when he took office. Al-Qaeda's leadership remained ensconced along the forbidding terrain of the tribal border region. Extremist militants threatened to expand their hold over territories in Pakistan's northwest, the Pakistani national economy had tumbled, and a new civilian government in Islamabad was seeking to assert itself after nearly a decade of military rule. Pakistan's efforts to confront extremism and insurgency remained weak and were applied inconsistently. The reverberations of the November 2008 Mumbai terrorist attacks were still being felt, illustrated by heightened tensions between India and Pakistan.

In Afghanistan, Taliban influence was on the rise and momentum had shifted against the international coalition and the Kabul government. Violence, including Afghan civilian casualties, had reached levels not seen since the initial U.S. invasion after 9/11. The Kabul government's weaknesses and corruption contributed to the Taliban resurgence, and the ANSF lacked the resources necessary to improve recruitment, training, and operational capacity.

Almost two years into the Obama administration, many of the underlying challenges of the region persist. Aggressive U.S. counterterror operations have degraded al-Qaeda and the Taliban leadership, but the most senior members of the organization remain at large and the group still threatens American security. Afghanistan's military, political, and economic challenges have been stubbornly intractable.

Critical counterinsurgency operations have been undertaken in southern Afghanistan but have proceeded more slowly and at greater cost than was initially anticipated. Allied efforts to build the ANSF have been injected with new resources and leadership but remain a work in progress. Afghanistan's deeply flawed presidential election in fall 2009 tarnished the Karzai government and contributed to an already difficult relationship between Washington and Kabul. The dark cloud of official corruption and the weakness of Afghan state institutions continue to fuel the Taliban cause. President Karzai is an uncertain partner. And throughout the entire period, the toll of U.S. and allied casualties has accelerated.

Pakistan has taken costly, commendable steps to fight select insurgents along the Afghan border, but its efforts against terrorist groups that threaten Afghanistan, India, and the United States—especially elements of the Afghan Taliban and LeT—have so far been lacking. Elements of Pakistan's security apparatus continue to distinguish between militant groups, considering some a strategic asset against India and others a hedge against turmoil in Afghanistan. Islamabad's relations with New Delhi have improved at the margins, but sparks between Pakistan and India could be reignited all too easily. Pakistan's economy and political stability continue to labor under severe stress.

The devastating floods have compounded the problems facing Islamabad. In the near term, much of Pakistan's energy will be consumed with meeting basic requirements for feeding, housing, and providing medical assistance to the internally displaced. Pakistan's military will be stretched thin by disaster management and will be therefore unlikely to focus on counterterror and counterinsurgency operations with the intensity of the preceding year. To achieve stability for Pakistan's large and growing population, post-flood reconstruction efforts must go well beyond repairing and rebuilding the crumbling infrastructure that existed prior to the disaster.

JUDGING PROGRESS

To continue the current course in Pakistan and Afghanistan, and the sacrifices it entails, progress must be visible and timely. In the absence of sustained progress, the relative costs and benefits of the current approach, compared with a scaled-down mission, will need to be recalculated. The crucial question is how Americans should assess progress.

In the short to medium term, Pakistan's floods will strain its national capacity to the limit. Islamabad's priorities will necessarily start with disaster recovery and reconstruction. The United States must continue to lead the world's response. If Islamabad is swamped by the sheer scale of the disaster, backsliding on security efforts is likely.

Even as Islamabad grapples with the floods and their aftermath, it will still face decisions about its own insurgency and how to deal with militants who threaten U.S. interests, including LeT and elements of the Afghan Taliban responsible for attacks on U.S. forces. It will be difficult to justify continued military assistance if Islamabad chooses to nurture or harbor these groups. Areas hit hardest by the floods have also been historic hotbeds for militancy. How Islamabad manages flood assistance to populations in Pakistan's northwest and the tribal belt along the Afghan border, recently ravaged by the man-made disaster of insurgency, will be important.

Americans should also be concerned about how the government deals with the Punjabi heartland, where the role of LeT affiliates and sympathizers poses a threat to Pakistan, India, and increasingly the United States. It must be clear to both Americans and Pakistanis that a successful attack against the U.S. homeland by one of these groups would deal a debilitating blow to the U.S.-Pakistan partnership. The United States needs to help Pakistan respond to the flood crisis in ways that win public confidence rather than play to the advantage of militant groups.

With respect to Afghanistan, the next U.S. strategic review is scheduled to begin in December 2010. The review should be a thorough assessment of whether sufficient progress is being made overall to conclude that the strategy is working. Progress will be difficult—but necessary—to measure. The Obama administration must address such issues as the capacity of the ANSF; the momentum of the Taliban in contested areas; the extent to which normal life is starting to return in recently secured territories; progress in building local security and civilian capacity; and the seriousness with which the Kabul government is fighting corruption in its own ranks.

President Obama has said that the United States will continue its present military surge until July 2011. If the review determines that progress is being made, the United States should then withdraw troops steadily on a district-by-district basis as conditions warrant, in line with the president's expressed intentions. However, if the review concludes that the current strategy is not working, a shift to a more limited mission at substantially reduced levels of forces would be warranted. The president's review should extend into 2011 if additional time is required to reach a firm assessment.

STRATEGIC OPTIONS

There are several strategic options available to the United States if the administration concludes that the current strategy is not working. In Pakistan, Washington could turn away from its present emphasis on rewarding and encouraging long-term bilateral cooperation. Instead, it could undertake increasingly aggressive, unilateral U.S. military strikes against Pakistan-based terrorists deeper into Pakistani territory, coercive diplomacy and sanctions, or a range of financial, diplomatic, and legal restrictions to control the flow of people, money, goods, and information to and from Pakistan. This strategy of containment and coercion could be coupled with a distinct diplomatic "tilt" toward India, with New Delhi serving as Washington's main strategic and counterterror partner in the region.

In Afghanistan, an alternative to the present U.S. counterinsurgency strategy would be a shift to smaller, highly mobile counterterror units backed by extensive surveillance and airpower assets. Washington could provide assistance to a range of Afghan allies, including what remains of the Kabul government as well as various local partners, in exchange for counterterror cooperation. It could be more forward-leaning in negotiations with the Taliban. Such a strategy would reduce the costs of war. Washington's emphasis would be on managing terrorist threats more than on investing in sustainable Afghan options.

These alternatives carry their own risks. In Pakistan, a shift to sticks without carrots is likely to result in a sharp backlash and is unlikely to encourage greater cooperation by Pakistan to address U.S. interests. A more hard-line approach would probably destabilize Pakistan, solidify popular anti-American sentiment, and fuel U.S.-Pakistan conflict over the long run. Engagement, partnership, and investment—with markers of progress—in support of common objectives are more apt to encourage desirable results.

In Afghanistan, a light-footprint strategy has some significant disadvantages. U.S. forces would operate in a deteriorating security environment, with fewer sympathetic Afghan partners. There would be fewer forces able to partner with Afghan troops, the best way to improve their capacity. U.S. forces could find it harder to move around the country to collect intelligence and to attack the enemy. A light footprint could increase the risk of a renewed Afghan civil war, a war that would have the potential to spiral into a regional proxy conflict, placing stress on an already overtaxed Pakistani state. A light footprint would still require thousands of U.S. troops to remain in Afghanistan under increasingly inhospitable conditions.

With these considerations in mind, strategic choices must be made based on a serious assessment of their relative costs and benefits. The United States must be prepared to consider other options if present efforts fail to demonstrate enough progress to justify their high costs.

RECOMMENDATIONS

Washington's first order of business in Pakistan must be to help address the extreme humanitarian suffering and dislocation caused by this summer's floods. If Pakistan cannot cope with the crisis, it cannot hope to tackle other threats to internal, regional, or international security. In general, the best way for the United States to address the challenges of terrorism and nuclear security in Pakistan is by working shoulder to shoulder with a stable partner in Islamabad.

To reinforce U.S.-Pakistan ties and contribute to Pakistan's economic stability in the aftermath of an overwhelming natural disaster, the Obama administration should prioritize—and the Congress should enact—an agreement that would grant preferential market access to Pakistani textiles. This agreement would help revive a devastated Pakistani industry and all of the associated sectors of the economy, including Pakistan-grown cotton. To further enhance Pakistan's stability, the United States should maintain current levels of economic and technical assistance to help military and civilian leaders reconstruct and establish control over areas hard-hit by the flood, including those contested by militant forces. American assistance should also encourage private-sector investment in conflict-prone and flood-ravaged regions. To build Pakistani support for the U.S.-Pakistan relationship, the United States must move rapidly to implement high-profile assistance projects and should also reach out on a sustained basis to nontraditional allies in Pakistani society, including business interests, educators, local media, and nongovernmental organizations (NGOs).

As it cultivates a closer partnership with Islamabad and contributes to shoring up the Pakistani state and national economy, the United States still needs to seek a shift in Pakistani strategic calculations about the use of militancy as a foreign policy tool. Washington should continue to make clear to Islamabad that, at a basic level, U.S. partnership and assistance depend upon action against LeT, the Afghan Taliban, especially the Haqqani network, and related international terror groups. These are the bedrock requirements for U.S. partnership and assistance over the long run.

By demonstrating American generosity and assistance at a time of grave Pakistani peril, the United States will also make a better case for the strategic benefits of its partnership. The U.S. government should simultaneously continue to strengthen its own capacity to collect intelligence on these groups, and should work to undermine their ability to harm American, Afghan, and Indian interests. Washington should ramp up its cooperation with other influential regional states, particularly China and Saudi Arabia, to coordinate its message to Islamabad on these issues.

To reduce regional tensions that distract from counterterror operations and undermine Pakistan's stability, the United States should
encourage progress in the Indo-Pakistani relationship. Washington
should not attempt to impose itself in Indo-Pakistani negotiations. An
indirect approach is better. The United States should help to build new
constituencies for peace by helping to fund international development
schemes that benefit businesses and people on both sides of the Indo-
Pakistani border.

In Afghanistan, core American security aims can best be achieved
at a lower cost if the United States manages to shift a greater burden to
Afghan partners. The present U.S. campaign requires a wider base of
local and national political support than the Karzai government and its
institutions are able to deliver. Worse, the popular backlash against government institutions, perceived as ineffective, corrupt, or even predatory, fuels the Taliban's resurgence. To address this major obstacle to
stability, the United States should encourage an initiative with three
complementary elements: political reform, national reconciliation, and
regional diplomacy.

Political reforms should aim to grant a greater voice to a broader
range of Afghan interests, such as local and provincial leaders, political
parties, and the parliament. Reforms will complement ongoing efforts
to fight corruption and improve the capacity of the Afghan government. In particular, these reforms should constitute the foundations for
effectively managing relations with President Karzai. The reform process will face political resistance, not least from President Karzai, but
the United States should use the leverage of its assistance and military
presence to help drive reforms through the Afghan political system. At
the same time, Washington should use its influence to press for Afghanistan's opposition leaders and important minority interests to play a
role in ongoing efforts at reconciliation with insurgents. These groups
will share Washington's core interest in avoiding a return of international terrorists or the ruthless Taliban regime of the past. Rather than
leaving the reconciliation process to President Karzai and his narrow
support base, Washington should participate fully in guiding a broad-
based, inclusive process, bearing in mind that a rapid breakthrough
at the negotiating table is unlikely. Afghan reform and reconciliation
should then be supported by a regional diplomatic accord brokered by
the United States.

To foster Afghanistan's viability as a security partner, the United States must continue to build cost-effective Afghan security forces appropriate to the capabilities necessary to protect the population. This will require more army and police trainers, as well as an expansion of community-based stabilization forces.

Afghanistan needs a self-sustaining foundation for generating jobs and revenue that will reduce dependence on international assistance. To meet this need, the United States should encourage private-sector investment in Afghanistan's considerable mineral and energy resources, in its agricultural sector, and in the infrastructure needed to expand trans-Afghan trade.

The Threat

To assess U.S. objectives in Pakistan and Afghanistan, it is necessary to understand the realities on the ground in the region. The range of immediate and long-term dangers is daunting. It includes terrorism, extremism, weak and corrupt governments, poverty, nuclear weapons, and deep-seated regional rivalries. Many current trends are likely to worsen over time. Each of these challenges is explored in detail in this report.

Many—but not all—of the most dangerous threats from Pakistan and Afghanistan are interconnected. In particular, the threat of militancy has been exported in both directions across their shared border for decades. Members of the Pakistani Taliban now seek sanctuary in Afghanistan, just as members of the Afghan Taliban have established sanctuaries in Pakistan. Each side has already suffered from the insecurity of the other, fueling tensions and mutual suspicions. Should Afghanistan relapse into civil war, it could become a battleground for regional hostilities, especially between India and Pakistan. Should Pakistan descend into greater internal disorder, the violence would spill into Afghanistan and spoil its prospects for peace and development.

The stakes for regional and global security are therefore exceedingly high.

PAKISTAN

That Pakistan has made some important, positive strides in recent years is often unappreciated. Its civil society and media have demonstrated an impressive capacity for political and social activism, illustrated by the lawyer-led protests that spurred the return of civilian rule to Islamabad in 2008. Progress has also been achieved in the fight against extremism. An overwhelming majority of Pakistanis have come to appreciate the need for army operations against the Pakistani Taliban based along the western border with Afghanistan. It is all too easy to forget how implausible this shift would have seemed just a few short years ago.

Yet at the time of this writing, Pakistan is confronting an unimaginable natural disaster with direct and immediate implications for tens of millions of its citizens. The immediate humanitarian suffering from the recent floods will gradually give way to the longer-term challenges of recovery and reconstruction. How Pakistan copes with this burden will influence its capacity in many other areas as well, including the fight against extremism and militancy. Such fragility in a country of Pakistan's size is a challenge of global proportions.

TERRORISM

Pakistan is already one of the world's most significant bases of international terrorism. U.S. military and intelligence efforts have dealt substantial blows to al-Qaeda's command and control capacity in Pakistan, particularly over the past year. Many of these operations have been conducted in cooperation with Pakistani officials.[3] Al-Qaeda and related groups hide in remote and difficult terrain, especially along the mountainous border with Afghanistan. Others seek refuge in Pakistan's teeming cities, like Karachi, home to roughly eighteen million Pakistanis. Karachi's estimated three million Pashtuns make it the largest urban Pashtun community in the world. These terrorist havens are often difficult to penetrate, but they are not isolated. Pakistan's telecommunications, financial, and transportation networks provide terrorists international reach. Those networks also make it hard to choke access to financial resources and recruits.

Pakistan is an attractive terrorist hub for at least three additional reasons. First, in Pakistan, terrorists find communities of sympathizers among a public that, for decades, has been inundated with extremist rhetoric and ideology. Islamist parties and sectarian groups are active throughout Pakistan's cities and institutions of higher education. Tribes along the Afghan border have offered sanctuary and support to terrorists for reasons of shared antipathy to the United States and its allies, customary hospitality, financial interest, and fear. Anti-Americanism remains rampant. Today the poisonous political climate offers little incentive for Pakistan's leaders, even when they do recognize the threat extremists pose, to work openly with Americans.

Second, Pakistan has a long history of officially sponsored militancy. In the 1980s, this strategy served short-term U.S. purposes. During the anti-Soviet jihad of the 1980s, Pakistan's intelligence service was the primary conduit between the U.S. Central Intelligence Agency (CIA) and the Afghan mujahedeen fighters. Many Pakistanis continue to view past U.S. support for these groups as the cause of Pakistan's present instability.

But today U.S. and Pakistani perspectives on militancy diverge in important ways. The connections between the Pakistani state and extremist militants persisted long after the Soviet Union collapsed and the United States left the scene. Pakistan differentiates between militant groups, now fighting vigorously against the Pakistani Taliban—which threatens the state—while offering support or turning a blind eye to those groups that direct violence against India, Afghanistan, the United States, and other targets outside Pakistan.

The reasons for this policy appear to be diverse. Some influential elements within Pakistan's military and intelligence services hold extreme ideologies. It is difficult, if not impossible, for outsiders to know how significant these circles of radical officers are. Other Pakistani officials still believe that militants can be controlled and used to further Pakistan's strategic interests in the region. In particular, they see militancy as a necessary tool for dealing with India, Pakistan's larger and increasingly formidable neighbor. For them, Afghanistan is a critical battleground for conflicting Indo-Pakistani interests. By providing sanctuary to Afghan militants, they believe they can influence events in Afghanistan, particularly after international forces withdraw.

Whatever the rationale, Pakistan's apparent strategy of distinguishing between various militant outfits is dangerous. It contradicts Washington's regional and global security efforts. Cross-border attacks against U.S. forces based in Afghanistan (conducted by the Haqqani network, Hizb-i Islami Gulbuddin, and the Quetta Shura Taliban) could be sharply reduced if the Pakistani army closed the bases of such groups inside Pakistan.

The expanding global reach and ambition of LeT, a group composed mainly of ethnic Pakistani Punjabis with strong historical links to the

Pakistani intelligence community and to al-Qaeda, makes it especially threatening. LeT is becoming a globalized terror network. Hubs and operatives across South Asia are linked to logistical, fund-raising, and recruiting networks in the Persian Gulf, and they have found supporters and sympathizers in the West—including in Britain, Canada, and the United States.[4] The U.S. director of national intelligence has testified that LeT "is becoming more of a direct threat, and is placing Western targets in Europe in its sights."[5] Left unchecked, LeT and its affiliates could eventually rival al-Qaeda as the world's most sophisticated and dangerous terrorist organization.

LeT's November 2008 attack in Mumbai offers a recent example of how Pakistan-based terrorists threaten American citizens and could spark a dangerous war between nuclear-armed India and Pakistan. Numerous Pakistan-based groups remain motivated and able to strike Indian targets again. Indian military restraint cannot be taken for granted in the event of another attack. Escalated tensions between New Delhi and Islamabad would compromise U.S. aims by shifting Islamabad's attention and resources away from operations against militants along its western border to defend against potential Indian retaliation along its eastern border. An Indo-Pakistani conflict could also disrupt the U.S. war effort in Afghanistan by cutting off Pakistan's vital supply corridors through which some three-quarters of all NATO supplies travel.

The final reason Pakistan remains a terrorist haven is that the state has struggled to impose its authority even when its leaders have decided to take on terrorists and insurgents. Between 2001 and 2010, Pakistan endured the deaths of nearly 2,300 soldiers, mainly in operations along the Afghan border.[6] Over the past several years, the army and frontier scouts have improved their capacity for clearing well-defended militant strongholds, but they have a much harder time sustaining these gains without effective civilian institutions to step in and administer law and order or provide access to basic services. Weak or nonexistent police forces and limited judicial facilities may be contributing to a reported problem of extrajudicial killings by Pakistani troops in areas once held by the Taliban.[7] Under these conditions, there is reason to fear that heavy-handed Pakistani military operations are as likely to create new local grievances as to root out entrenched militant networks.

WEAK INSTITUTIONS

When it comes to assessing Pakistan's future, these immediate military challenges pale in comparison to the enormous task of holding the line against extremism and militancy within Pakistani society. Pakistan's civilian institutions, especially the judiciary and the police force, are too often weak and corrupt.[8] For most Pakistanis, economic survival is a challenge, security is poor, and justice is slow. These failures of the state alienate the public and energize extremists. Worse still, Pakistan's FATA along the Afghan border are governed under a system of limited tribal autonomy inherited from the British that was never intended to provide the administrative features of a modern state. The structures that exist have been strained by decades of conflict. Militants have exploited this power vacuum, often by killing off tribal elders and imposing their own authority.

The weakness of Pakistan's public institutions raises serious questions about the long-term stability of the state. Pakistan's floods will compound its challenges, diverting already scarce resources from much-needed infrastructure investments to humanitarian response, recovery, and rehabilitation. Instead of getting ahead, Pakistan must now struggle harder to stop falling further behind. Rapid population growth—projected to reach three hundred million by mid-century—will place additional stress on national resources. At present, two-thirds of Pakistanis live on less than $2 a day. Potable water, energy, food, and land will become scarcer. Pakistan's cities pose special challenges. For example, Karachi—which contributes up to 60 percent of the national economy—is stressed by rapid population growth and riven by political and ethnic cleavages. Ineffective civilian institutions will be unable to educate Pakistan's people, build public infrastructure, or keep the peace.

Without injections of foreign assistance or far more rapid economic growth, Pakistan will be unable to create the estimated two million new jobs per year required to keep a lid on unemployment.[9] Under those conditions, an enormous youth population (today nearly 60 percent of Pakistanis are younger than twenty-four) will be more susceptible to extreme ideologies and antistate violence.

Pakistan's tumultuous politics, rising and falling between civilian and military rule, are partly to blame for the weak performance of its administrators and leaders. Political uncertainty and upheaval have also reduced economic growth by discouraging private investment. Pakistan's latest political transition, starting with national elections in February 2008, has not yet produced a full democratic consolidation. After President Musharraf left office, the army quickly retreated from the foreground of Pakistani politics, but a close examination reveals that it continues to call the shots on all important issues of national defense and foreign policy. Pakistan's political class has been too consumed with partisan skirmishing and the massive challenges of the civil sector to mount a serious threat to military authority. For the time being, the Pakistani army appears content with its autonomy and shows little inclination for a formal reentry into the political fray.

NUCLEAR WEAPONS

Finally, Pakistan's nuclear arsenal, estimated to house between eighty and one hundred weapons, sets it apart from all other states that confront an active Islamist insurgency. Pakistan and the United States have never seen eye to eye on the Pakistani nuclear program. Those differences forced a rupture in the relationship throughout the 1990s, when congressionally mandated sanctions ended U.S. military sales and assistance to Pakistan. Subsequently, the extensive nuclear smuggling ring, led by the so-called father of Pakistan's nuclear program, Abdul Qadeer Khan, raised new fears in Washington. Contemplating the terrible prospect that nuclear materials could fall into the hands of a sophisticated terrorist group like al-Qaeda, the George W. Bush administration quietly established a nuclear security assistance program for Pakistan, which continues to this day. President Obama has publicly expressed his confidence that Pakistan's nuclear program is secure, but the Task Force remains deeply concerned by Pakistan's unique combination of the world's most sophisticated terrorist groups and what appears to be the world's fastest growing nuclear program.[10]

For its part, the vast majority of the Pakistani public sees the nuclear arsenal as a necessary safeguard against India. Pakistan seeks international acceptance of its nuclear status but, like India, remains an outlier from the Nuclear Nonproliferation Treaty (NPT) regime. Pakistan continues to expand its nuclear program in an effort to equalize India's conventional military superiority. Islamabad has repeatedly expressed misgivings over the recent U.S.-India civil nuclear deal and has requested a similar special status. Pakistanis tend to argue that U.S. nuclear policy reflects a double standard and a tilt toward India. Differences over nuclear issues continue to hinder U.S.-Pakistan cooperation and contribute to the lack of trust between the two sides.

AFGHANISTAN

In the first few years after 9/11, U.S. military and intelligence operations succeeded in forcing al-Qaeda and a number of other international terrorist groups out of Afghanistan. The repressive Taliban regime in Kabul was toppled, and most Afghans, especially those in the north and west, welcomed international assistance and the new opportunity for peace and growth.

Since 2006, however, there has been a rising tide of Taliban violence. Afghanistan's ability to create conditions for sustainable security—without a substantial outside presence—will remain a principal challenge to U.S. goals in the region. A military victory by the Taliban in southern and eastern Afghanistan could embolden international terrorists along the Afghanistan-Pakistan border. Although some Afghan Taliban leaders appear willing to distance themselves from al-Qaeda and other international terrorists, other elements—especially the Haqqani network based in Pakistan's North Waziristan Agency—have embraced the ideology, rhetoric, and tactics of al-Qaeda's global jihad. Afghanistan's remote geography, difficult terrain, and militant history make it an especially appealing destination for these groups. Perceptions of extremist victories in Afghanistan could energize radical movements around the world.

Afghanistan is not yet capable of standing on its own. The post-Taliban rebuilding process started from an extremely low base. Decades of war had destroyed civilian and military institutions, deprived young Afghans of education, and sent many of the country's most talented people into exile. Today, Afghan government spending on development and security programs far exceeds domestic revenues. International donors provide approximately 70 percent of the Afghan government-administered budget.[11] Poor international coordination has also hindered reconstruction since 2002. The inability of the international community—in particular, the United Nations (UN)—to harmonize political and development efforts among international donors has wasted precious resources and fueled frustration among many Afghans.

NATO's failure to share the burden of Afghanistan among its members has limited the effectiveness of its forces. Over the past nine years, many NATO troop contributors have circumscribed the ways in which their troops can be used. Most are now looking to reduce, not expand, their combat roles.

Previous efforts to train and equip the ANSF faced routine shortfalls in resources and qualified trainers. To different degrees, these forces have suffered from high attrition rates and corrupt practices. In many cases, the underpaid, unsupervised, and poorly trained police force has preyed upon the public more than protected it. NATO is now expanding the ANSF rapidly and at great cost. Recent reports suggest that the ANA monthly attrition rate is falling and that weapons training is increasingly effective. From November 2009 to June 2010, the monthly attrition rate of the ANA dropped from 3 percent to 1.2 percent. The number of Afghan soldiers graduating from NATO basic training who qualified on their primary weapon rose from 35 percent to 65 percent.[12] The Afghan army and national police accomplished their October 2010 goals by reaching a force size of 134,000 and 109,000, respectively, in late August 2010.[13] To help tackle Afghanistan's urgent security needs, NATO has also worked to overcome official Afghan objections to organizing and assisting local defense forces.[14]

POLITICAL AND ECONOMIC WEAKNESS

On the political front, Afghanistan's weaknesses are even more apparent. In many parts of the country, the state is missing in action. Insurgents and local power brokers have exploited the vacuum, asserting their authority and winning some measure of public legitimacy. In other instances, especially in southern Afghanistan, the Kabul government is itself perceived as a cause of insecurity. Widespread official corruption and predatory practices have turned many Afghans against their own government and created opportunities for a Taliban resurgence. If the United States lends its support to state authorities without first demanding more effective governance, it risks alienating local communities and sparking a violent backlash.

Although the first presidential election in October 2004 was an uplifting national experience, the second attempt five years later was a

fiasco that weakened the legitimacy of President Karzai and his government and eroded the international community's confidence in Kabul.
After four sets of national elections, it is clear that Afghanistan still
lacks basic mechanisms—like a credible system for voter registration—
required for sustaining its democratic process at a reasonable cost over
the long term.

The quality of Afghanistan's national ministries varies widely, but
all suffer from a shortage of qualified, honest officials willing to work
under difficult conditions for the low wages on offer. Provincial and
district governments are dominated by unelected officials, including
governors and police chiefs, appointed by President Karzai. Karzai's
dependence on major power brokers, including his brother, fuels a
political system that is nominally democratic but, in practice, unac-
countable to local demands. Afghanistan's constitutional and electoral
structures have obstructed the formation of effective political party
organizations. Without political parties, the parliament lacks discipline
and is less effective than it needs to be. Where the government fails, the
Taliban offers an alternative and gains public legitimacy. At the local
level, the Taliban is especially adept at exploiting the weaknesses of the
formal justice system. Unlike government courts, the Taliban dispenses
quick, efficient rulings backed by force.

Without Afghan political partners and substantial national acceptance of the government in Kabul, the United States cannot hope to
bring enduring stability to Afghanistan. However, Afghanistan's
political weaknesses are not intrinsic. Last year's presidential elections
demonstrated that Afghanistan has a multitude of energetic and skill-
ful politicians. Decades of war and external intervention should not
obscure the fact that from 1929 until the Soviet invasion in 1979, the
country was at peace.[15] Many local communities throughout the country adhere to traditional forms of representative governance. Far from
seeking Afghanistan's breakup into ethnic enclaves, the vast majority
of Afghans favors national unity and accepts the basic tenets of plural-
istic rule.

Today, however, Afghanistan lacks the economic growth that would
permit it to sustain government revenues and reduce the appeal of illicit
activities, like narcotics and smuggling. High levels of violence dampen
foreign investment and licit trade. Although recent announcements of
vast mineral and energy deposits may offer opportunities for growth,
the experience of other weak states endowed with valuable resources

provides a cautionary tale; such wealth can too easily fuel internal conflict and external exploitation.[16] Afghanistan's single largest outside investment—China's stake in the Aynak copper mine south of Kabul—is years away from creating jobs or revenues.[17] U.S. efforts to support Afghanistan's agricultural sector could help millions of Afghans plant crops other than opium poppy, but ambitious farmers will also require greater access to regional markets. For too long, Pakistani barriers to trade and transit have obstructed Afghan exports to India. Islamabad has only recently concluded a deal to permit the entry of Afghan trucks en route to India.[18] Similar political conflicts and concerns about instability undercut proposals for energy pipelines from Iran or Central Asia to Pakistan and India.

RECONCILIATION

Under the assumption that many Afghan insurgent leaders are motivated less by extreme ideologies than by political goals or personal grievances, the Karzai government is pursuing what it calls a reconciliation dialogue with top Taliban commanders in an attempt to end the civil conflict without military force. Facing a sometimes strained relationship with Washington and uncertain support from within his own Pashtun constituency, President Karzai may also see reconciliation as the best means to salvage his political fortunes. This Task Force is concerned that "reconciliation" is not being pursued in a way that builds greater Afghan unity. Negotiations have already exposed rifts in the Kabul government. Afghan minorities and women's groups will be especially concerned about any deal that would return extremists to positions of authority. A poorly managed negotiation process would also create divisions between Kabul and Washington and among the NATO allies.

Whatever its prospects, the reconciliation process will be watched closely by Afghanistan's neighbors, all of whom feel that they will be profoundly affected by developments in Kabul. Pakistan already appears to be using its ties to Afghan Taliban leaders to shape the process and reduce Indian influence. In return, India and other regional players are particularly sensitive to Pakistani power plays. All of Afghanistan's neighbors may already be hedging their bets in anticipation of a return to Afghan civil war. Renewed competition for influence in Afghanistan has the potential to rip the country apart, despite the fact that each state in the region would benefit far more from a period of peace and stability. Afghans would again suffer the most, with millions of refugees streaming across the borders into Pakistan, Iran, and elsewhere. Pakistan and the Central Asian Republics, already fragile, would be especially threatened by the turmoil of a renewed proxy war in Afghanistan. Moreover, the world would suffer if Afghanistan's internal conflict permits a return of al-Qaeda and other international terrorists.

Unfortunately, regional powers like China, Iran, and Russia have tended to see Afghanistan as Washington's problem more than their own. They perceive their security threats narrowly. For instance, Beijing stresses the threat posed by Uighur separatists, Russia directs its gaze at Caucasian and Central Asian terrorists, and Iran raises concerns about narcotics trafficking. Rather than making significant contributions to Afghan stability overall, they each tend to pursue minimalist economic and political agendas.

U.S. Strategic Objectives

The basic long-term U.S. aspirations for Pakistan and Afghanistan are uncontroversial and easy to list: stability, prosperity, and good governance. The more important—and more difficult—challenge is to identify U.S. goals that are realistically achievable within a reasonable time frame, taking into account the immense challenges of the region and the limits of U.S. power. The central question is not what the United States might wish to achieve but what it should aim to accomplish.

Since 9/11, U.S. goals in Pakistan and Afghanistan have shifted in important but often unappreciated ways. Over this period, the United States has not always been clear enough about its specific goals and timelines. It is necessary to be realistic about precisely what Washington should seek to accomplish, with what resources, and for how long.

SHIFTING U.S. OBJECTIVES IN PAKISTAN

U.S. aims in Pakistan have shifted over the past decade. The United States viewed its aims in narrow terms immediately after 9/11: Pakistan was a necessary element of the military and counterterror campaign in Afghanistan. Washington demanded that Islamabad cut its ties to the Taliban–al-Qaeda alliance in Afghanistan and serve as the U.S. staging ground and logistics hub.[19] As it became ever more apparent to the George W. Bush administration that the terrorist threat had roots in Pakistan's tribal areas and cities, the United States adopted a broader definition of its objectives. It made significant efforts to shore up the Pakistani economy and strengthen military and intelligence ties. It began a quiet dialogue and assistance program to address Pakistan's nuclear security issues. By 2005, U.S. leaders had begun to place more emphasis on Pakistan's internal politics, broadening their focus from Pakistan's connections to Afghanistan and the U.S. counterterror mission. The goal of supporting a Pakistani transition to civilian rule was widely debated. Tough questions were raised about how to square the Bush administration's security aims with its commitment to democracy promotion.

As the Obama administration came into office, Pakistan was in the midst of an uncertain transition to civilian rule. At the same time, terrorist violence and militancy spiked, jarring the Pakistani public and raising new fears about the state's ability to assert control over its territory. Together, these developments led Obama administration officials and the Congress to undertake an even more expansive commitment to partnership with Pakistan.[20] Far from the narrow agenda of 2001, Washington expressed broad security, economic, and political objectives, ranging from democratic consolidation and poverty alleviation to regional stability and improved counterinsurgency capacity. Reflecting this agenda, the Obama administration has undertaken a broad and energetic engagement with the Pakistani government and military, embodied in a "strategic dialogue" that cuts across both governments' bureaucracies.

SHIFTING U.S. OBJECTIVES IN AFGHANISTAN

U.S. aims in Afghanistan have also shifted over time. The United States did not make a premeditated choice to focus its attention and resources on the small, landlocked state. Al-Qaeda's attacks on the United States spurred that shift. The initial goal of U.S. military operations in Afghanistan was narrowly conceived: to eliminate the threat posed by al-Qaeda. The mission was urgent and not preceded by extensive long-term planning. It is possible that if top al-Qaeda leaders had been apprehended and brought to justice within weeks or months after 9/11, U.S. forces would have withdrawn from Afghanistan, especially as the Bush administration prepared for war in Iraq.

Although U.S. efforts did not produce rapid results in the hunt for Osama bin Laden, they did make quick work of the Taliban regime in Kabul. The longer the United States stayed in Afghanistan, the more blurry the line became between its narrow counterterror mission and a more ambitious effort to build a post-Taliban Afghan state. Afghan leaders and the international community created a road map for the creation of new democratic institutions, U.S. assistance helped to expand the Afghan education system, and extensive investments were made in roads and other physical infrastructure. Each of these efforts suggested aspirations far broader than counterterrorism.

By the time President Obama moved into the White House and began his first strategic review, the war in Afghanistan had taken a serious turn for the worse. The euphoria of Afghanistan's first democratic elections had given way to disillusionment and a rising Taliban insurgency. In response, the Obama administration sought to rein in public expectations. Secretary of Defense Robert M. Gates testified before the Senate Armed Services Committee in January 2009 that U.S. goals in Afghanistan should be "modest" and "realistic." He added, "If we set ourselves the objective of creating some sort of Central Asian Valhalla over there, we will lose, because nobody in the world has that kind of time, patience, and money."[21]

At the U.S. Military Academy at West Point in December 2009, after the Obama administration's second policy review, the president reaffirmed the overarching objective he had articulated earlier that year, to "disrupt, dismantle, and defeat" al-Qaeda, and to prevent its ability to threaten America and its allies from a sanctuary in the region. The Obama administration has recognized, however, that it will be difficult to deny al-Qaeda and related terrorist organizations the opportunity to restore and expand their base in Afghanistan unless the Taliban is weakened and the ability of the Afghan government to provide security and basic services is strengthened. The White House's rhetoric, however, often poses the mission in the narrowest terms—defeating al-Qaeda—without explaining to the American people how fighting the Taliban and building local capacity in Afghanistan support that counterterror mission and justify the surge strategy. This causes confusion and reduces public support for the effort.

REALISTIC ENDS, MEANS, AND TIMETABLES FOR PAKISTAN

This Task Force finds that the United States has two vital national security objectives in Pakistan: to degrade and defeat the terrorist groups that threaten U.S. interests from its territory and to prevent turmoil that would imperil the Pakistani state and risk the security of its nuclear program. It will be exceedingly difficult to achieve either of these objectives without the cooperation of the Pakistani state; this requires improving the quality of the U.S.-Pakistan relationship. By extension, Washington has an interest in the stability of its Pakistani partner, which includes the security of Pakistan's population, the health of its economy, the capacity of its governing institutions, and the character of its relations with other states in the region.

By any realistic assessment, Pakistan faces enormously difficult long-term challenges to its stability. As long as the troubling social, political, and economic dynamics outlined earlier in this report persist, Pakistan's door will be propped open to terrorism and insurgency. Fostering conditions for security, more effective democratic governance, and prosperity will require the efforts of millions of Pakistanis. Such a process cannot be imposed from the outside, even by a superpower, but it can and should be supported by U.S. assistance directed to committed Pakistani allies.

In the short run, Washington should focus on helping Pakistan through a terrible national tragedy. U.S. assistance will be essential for Pakistan to cope with the economic and human costs of the floods. If Pakistan manages to pull through this crisis without suffering a more significant political or social breakdown, that will be a success. By fully supporting that process, Washington has a chance to demonstrate to Pakistanis the material benefits of U.S. partnership as well as the generosity of the American people.

But to succeed over the long run, the U.S. relationship with Pakistan must be a two-way street. Washington should patiently offer incentives to build trust and confidence with Islamabad. But this assistance is not simply charity. It is an investment in Pakistan's future and the future of its partnership with the United States. To be a sound investment, it must continue to show a realistic potential for growth in terms of enhanced Pakistani cooperation on issues of importance to the United States—namely, a demonstrated effort to crack down on all terrorist groups based in its territory.

Washington's investments in Pakistan may never sway Islamabad's fundamental views. In that case, the United States should aim to change the methods by which Pakistan pursues its interests. For example, rather than suggest that Pakistan should no longer perceive a security threat from India or exercise influence in Afghanistan, Washington should encourage and enable Pakistan to pursue diplomatic and economic strategies in place of militarized approaches. This approach must be complemented by a harder edge: sustained U.S. efforts to weaken Pakistan-based terrorist groups and their sympathizers, including elements of the Afghan Taliban, al-Qaeda, and LeT. As these groups are diminished, they will pose less of a direct threat to U.S., Indian, or Afghan interests. They will become less relevant to Pakistan's own regional strategic calculations and more easily dismantled. At the same time, the United States should target its military assistance to Pakistan in ways that most effectively support Pakistan's counterinsurgency efforts at home.

The cultivation of effective, mutually beneficial relations with Pakistan is a means to achieve fundamental security goals. Washington must always place a higher priority on protecting the security of its citizens than on improving the bilateral relationship for its own sake. If there is a mass casualty attack against Americans that can be traced to Pakistan, or if U.S. policymakers grow frustrated by inadequate Pakistani efforts to address critical security issues, the partnership may founder. In that case (a scenario considered later in this report), the United States could be forced to scale back its aims, focusing instead on managing and containing immediate threats to U.S. security, especially those posed by international terrorist organizations like al-Qaeda.

At present, however, this Task Force believes that enhanced U.S.-Pakistan cooperation is both desirable and feasible, if by no means straightforward. The policy recommendations in this report are designed to improve prospects for achieving these ends in a timely manner.

REALISTIC ENDS, MEANS, AND TIMETABLES FOR AFGHANISTAN

The United States should pursue three main objectives in Afghanistan.

The first is to prosecute the war against al-Qaeda and other international terror organizations concentrated on the Afghanistan-Pakistan border, together with Pakistan where possible, unilaterally where not. The toxic network of extremist groups—which includes various elements of the Afghan Taliban, the Pakistani Taliban, and LeT—is difficult to disentangle and blurs the distinction between terrorism and insurgency. The specific agendas of these groups may differ, but they are increasingly united by operational ties and jihadist ideals.

At the same time, the United States needs to prevent Afghanistan from once again becoming a sanctuary for these groups. Al-Qaeda is now on the defensive in the border region as a result of relentless and effective U.S. drone strikes. But if the Taliban consolidates its position in large portions of Afghanistan, it could create new space for these dangerous groups to plan attacks against the United States and destabilize the region. If a combination of these groups were to succeed against the United States in Afghanistan, home of the earlier jihadist victory against the Soviet Union, it would be a rallying point for other extremist groups around the world.

Second, the United States should work to prevent Afghanistan from spiraling into a civil war, which would have a destabilizing effect on neighboring Pakistan and the region. Such a war would threaten already fragile Central Asian states and would almost certainly exacerbate Indo-Pakistani tensions. Because Washington seeks to improve its partnership with both New Delhi and Islamabad, the renewal of a bitter and violent proxy war between the two would represent a significant obstacle.

The decades of Soviet occupation and civil war in Afghanistan have already been costly for Pakistan. A renewed Afghan civil war would compound the problem. The war economy of gunrunning, narcotics, and militancy has contributed to Pakistan's own internal insurgency. Afghanistan's war has undermined Pakistani stability in other, more insidious ways as well. Pakistan's experience in Afghanistan during the 1980s was a formative one. Islamabad's support of the Afghan mujahedeen guerrillas enabled a vast expansion of Pakistan's Directorate for Inter-Services Intelligence (ISI). It also strengthened Pakistan's pattern of fomenting insurgency as a means to promote its regional interests. A military victory by the present Taliban insurgency would reinforce these lessons. Yet these same groups propagate jihadist ideas that endanger Pakistan's own stability. The Pakistani Taliban—a conglomeration of groups that have turned on Islamabad and challenged the writ of the state—is a prime example of this problem of strategic blowback.

Third, the United States should develop Afghan security forces capable of defending the population as the United States reduces its footprint and shifts its mission. Seeking to prevent extremist attacks and a destabilizing civil war cannot mean an open-ended, bloody U.S. military engagement—a "forever war."[22] To continue the current course in Pakistan and Afghanistan, and the sacrifices it entails, progress must be visible and timely. In the absence of sustainable progress, the relative costs and benefits of the current approach, compared with a scaled-down mission, need to be recalculated, and Washington should be prepared to adjust its strategy and policies without delay. That scenario is considered at greater length later in this report.

The implications of this constraint are clear: in order for the United States to accomplish its objectives in Afghanistan at an acceptable cost, it will need to encourage and enable Afghans and other regional states to shoulder greater responsibilities. This means securing their support for degrading the threat now posed by al-Qaeda and its affiliated Afghan militant groups, such as the Haqqani network; helping to support Afghan partners who can do more to build and maintain security with less direct U.S. military involvement; and working to craft political and diplomatic settlements in Afghanistan that reduce internal and regional tensions.

An Assessment of U.S. Strategy and Policy

Since taking office, President Obama has shifted U.S. strategies and dramatically expanded U.S. military and civilian commitments to Pakistan and Afghanistan. The Task Force supports these changes, with some important caveats and concerns.

CURRENT U.S. POLICY IN PAKISTAN

The Obama administration has embarked on a comprehensive approach to building a more effective partnership with Pakistan. It involves an aggressive counterterrorism strategy and a generous aid program. In October 2009, Congress, with presidential approval, passed the Enhanced Partnership with Pakistan Act (Kerry-Lugar-Berman), which pledged $7.5 billion in nonmilitary assistance over the next five years. This amounts to a tripling of assistance from prior levels. In July 2010, during her visit to Islamabad, Secretary of State Hillary Clinton announced plans to devote U.S. assistance funds to power, water, health care, finance, and postconflict reconstruction projects, among others.[23] These plans are likely to be revised in the aftermath of Pakistan's summer floods. To meet urgent humanitarian needs, Washington has already contributed food and relief supplies, as well as over $150 million in direct assistance.[24]

In March 2010, the first meeting of the U.S.-Pakistan Strategic Dialogue in Washington, DC, included numerous working groups that covered a wide range of issues. Among them, the Pakistani side put forward a request for a civil nuclear agreement similar to that between the United States and India. Washington correctly deflected the nuclear issue, focusing instead on Pakistan's need for greater power production and electricity distribution capacity. On the nuclear front, the United States has for years engaged in quiet, limited cooperation with

Pakistan's Strategic Plans Division, the unit of the military responsible for maintaining its nuclear arsenal. Although many Americans continue to harbor concerns about the terrorist threat to Pakistan's nuclear scientists, technologies, and materials, Pakistan has taken important steps to enhance security controls. At the same time, Pakistan appears to be expanding its nuclear program rapidly, a development that increases the potential for accidents and raises tensions with India. The United States has publicly raised concerns about China's recent plans to provide greater assistance to Pakistan's nuclear program, actions that appear to violate Beijing's voluntary obligations as a member of the Nuclear Suppliers Group.[25]

The United States is supporting a more aggressive Pakistani campaign against antistate militants. At more than $1.2 billion, U.S. assistance to Pakistan's security forces during the past year is on par with U.S. assistance to Egypt's security forces, and Pakistan ranks among the top five recipients of Washington's military aid.[26] It includes a combination of items useful for counterinsurgency operations as well as significant conventional warfare capabilities.[27] After losing access to a generation of Pakistani military leaders because of their exclusion from U.S. military educational programs, the Pentagon's efforts to build cooperation with Pakistan's military and intelligence services have yielded some encouraging results. Training and assistance for Pakistan's Frontier Corps have made a particularly constructive difference. That said, progress in building military-to-military relations is often slow, costly, and full of frustrations.

The United States has also greatly intensified direct military operations against terrorist camps in Pakistan. The monthly rate of publicly reported drone strikes in 2010 is double the 2009 rate.[28] Targeting has improved, reducing civilian casualties. Attacks along the Afghan border have struck militants from al-Qaeda, the Afghan Taliban, the Pakistani Taliban, and the Haqqani network. U.S. drones have eliminated several top terrorist leaders since January 2009, including the head of the Pakistani Taliban and al-Qaeda's chief operating officer.[29] The tactical success of these strikes has come at some cost in Pakistani public sentiment. A heated debate over civilian casualties and territorial sovereignty pulses over the airwaves there, but Pakistan's military and government request drone technologies for their own use more than they protest against the strikes. Quietly, many Pakistanis from the region bordering Afghanistan have expressed qualified support for drone attacks, noting that they are

more accurate than in the past, but are still frustrated that they are operated by the United States and not by Pakistan itself.

In the midst of persistent political dynamism, including the debate
and ultimate passage of Pakistan's eighteenth constitutional amend-
ment, which stripped President Asif Ali Zardari of many formal
powers, the United States has wisely attempted to cultivate a neutral
stance rather than backing any particular party or leader. This stance
has continued through several periods of Pakistani political upheaval.
But Pakistan's latest experiment with civilian rule has faltered in important ways, not least in its ineffective attempt to assert greater civilian
control over the army and intelligence services. Bowing to the reality
of the military's dominant role, the Obama administration has made
heavy use of its close working relationship with Pakistan's army chief to
manage sensitive strategic issues. In an apparent nod to his personal sig-
nificance, and perhaps his close U.S. ties, Pakistan army chief General
Ashfaq Parvez Kayani's term was recently extended by three years; it is
now set to expire in 2013.

The Task Force broadly endorses these new features of U.S. policy
in Pakistan. Looking ahead, several important challenges threaten
U.S. goals and the overall U.S.-Pakistan partnership, especially the
following:

– *Flood relief and reconstruction.* Unless Pakistan's civilian and military
  leadership manages to cope with this natural disaster, there will be
  little hope for meeting other political, economic, or security goals.

– *U.S. assistance implementation.* For the United States to help meet
  Pakistani needs in ways that contribute to a lasting partnership, new
  U.S. assistance projects must be rolled out with urgency, complemented by effective publicity. Plans for projects conceived before
  the floods will need to be reviewed immediately and revised to meet
  more pressing needs.

– *Trade barriers.* U.S. assistance, in itself, cannot reverse the fact that
  if current trends hold over the coming decades, most Pakistanis will
  remain young, poor, uneducated, and brimming with anti-Americanism. High U.S. tariffs on Pakistan's top export items limit the potential for commercial ties between the two countries. U.S. tariffs on
  Pakistan's leading exports, such as textiles, average about four times
  the U.S. tariff rate on imports from other countries. Since nearly 40
  percent of Pakistan's industrial employment is in textiles, it is likely

that millions of Pakistanis could benefit from greater access to the U.S. market for these goods.[30] Pakistan's cotton farmers could also gain a necessary boost in their attempt to recover from the floods.

– *Militant ties.* Pakistan has not made a decisive break with all militants on its territory, especially those active against India and Afghanistan. LeT and elements of the Afghan Taliban, including the Haqqani network, are still operating with the active or passive assistance of the Pakistani state and pose urgent challenges for U.S. efforts in Afghanistan and its counterterrorism efforts around the world. Pakistan's behavior appears to be motivated, at least in part, by its interest in maintaining influence in a post-NATO Afghanistan through links to the Taliban.

– *Nuclear concerns.* A deep trust deficit remains between Washington and Islamabad on nuclear security issues. U.S. efforts to assist Pakistan in safeguarding its weapons are constrained by U.S. law and Pakistani concerns that Washington seeks to "roll back" its program. China's nuclear assistance to Pakistan undermines the U.S. nonproliferation agenda, but Washington's concerns have so far been ignored.

– *India-Pakistan rivalry.* Continuing rivalry between India and Pakistan play out in Afghanistan as well as undercut efforts to encourage regional trade, investment, and security. Recent Indo-Pakistani meetings, including between foreign ministers, have been contentious at best.

– *Postconflict capacity.* Pakistani stability remains threatened by the limited capacity of its army, police, Frontier Corps, and other civilian administrators to successfully "hold" and "build" after counterinsurgency "clearing" operations in the FATA and Khyber-Pakhtunkhwa Province. These same areas have been especially hard-hit by floods, sweeping away recent investments in infrastructure and development.

– *Civil-military relations.* A recent period of relative political calm masks deeper tensions between Pakistan's military and its civilian politicians. In this respect, the latest attempt to consolidate civilian democracy is still a work in progress, with uncertain implications for national security.

– *Public opinion.* Negative Pakistani perceptions poison cooperation at all levels. Anti-American critics dominate Pakistan's airwaves.

CURRENT U.S. POLICY IN AFGHANISTAN

Since his inauguration, President Obama has conducted two major strategic reviews for Afghanistan. Together, these reviews endorsed a plan intended to disrupt, dismantle, and defeat al-Qaeda and allied groups in the region, and to prevent both Afghanistan and Pakistan from providing safe havens to international terrorists in the future. President Obama repeatedly declared his intention to make up for years of U.S. underinvestment in Afghanistan and announced major new deployments of troops, civilian officials, and other resources.

Current U.S. strategy is founded upon the belief that if the Taliban were to retake power, the United States could have little confidence in its desire or capacity to prevent al-Qaeda's return. The Task Force agrees that the United States cannot afford to underestimate the fact that elements of the Afghan Taliban with close ties to al-Qaeda, such as the Haqqani network and associated groups like LeT, are already active inside Afghanistan and would pose an even greater threat if they gained more operating space there. Rather than a war of attrition, Washington seeks to weaken the Taliban by depriving the insurgency of access to its sustaining lifeblood: men, money, and safe havens among sympathetic populations. These goals are possible because the Taliban is not particularly popular among Afghans. It has mainly proven adept at taking advantage of ethnic and tribal cleavages within Afghan society, popular grievances against the state, and the nationalistic frustration born of international military presence. The Taliban is also ruthless in its efforts to eliminate or intimidate opponents and to cow the rest of the population into acquiescence. By improving public security, creating new economic opportunities, and enhancing the quality of Afghan governance, the United States and its partners seek to diminish Taliban power and influence.

The Task Force finds that the Obama administration's strategy for Afghanistan may manage to turn the tide against the Taliban insurgency and reduce the risks of international terrorism. It holds out the prospect of building a stable Afghanistan without permanent U.S. or international security forces. However, these desirable outcomes will be difficult to achieve, even with the additional resources at hand. Washington's Afghanistan strategy will demand great sacrifices and will ultimately rise or fall on whether Afghanistan's people and leaders line up behind it.

Starting in spring 2009, Washington's strategy has been backed by a surge of U.S. forces to a total of one hundred thousand in late summer 2010. Over a similar time frame, U.S. Special Operations Forces have tripled their capacity.[31] A primary mission for NATO is to train Afghanistan's national army and police, but NATO has been able to field only slightly over half of the international trainers needed. So far, the United States has spent more than $26 billion to build the ANSF, and current plans would require $6 billion per year through 2015.[32] In July 2010, as part of a short-term effort to expand anti-Taliban forces, NATO convinced the Kabul government to permit the equipping, training, and organization of community defense forces under the authority of the interior ministry.[33]

A revamped civilian effort is also supporting the military surge. Since January 2009, the overall U.S. civilian presence has tripled to one thousand, while deployments outside Kabul have quadrupled.[34] The Obama administration has refocused economic assistance (more than $2.6 billion during the 2009–2010 fiscal year) to the agricultural sector, on which approximately 80 percent of Afghans rely for their livelihoods. In a revamped counternarcotics policy, the Obama administration has emphasized interdiction and "alternative livelihoods" programs aimed at targeting kingpins without angering farmers. The new approach is supported by an increase in U.S. Drug Enforcement Administration personnel and material, as well as technical assistance to farmers.[35]

Even as these major new commitments have been announced, President Obama has also pledged that the increased U.S. military commitment will not be open-ended. The United States will begin to transition lead responsibility for security to Afghan forces in July 2011, although the specific pace of that process will be determined by conditions on the ground in Afghanistan.[36] At the July 2010 Kabul conference, the parties expressed support for President Karzai's objective that the ANSF "should lead and conduct military operations in all provinces by the end of 2014."[37]

The geographic focus of the recent U.S. surge is Afghanistan's Pashtun south, the birthplace and stronghold of the Taliban movement. In NATO's spring 2010 drive to secure the Helmand River valley, Taliban fighters were dislodged from their sanctuary in the district of Marjah, and new local officials were installed. Months later, Taliban intimidation remains widespread. Marjah has shown the critical shortcomings of Afghan state capacity and the difficulty of "holding," "building," and "transferring" following the completion of initial military operations. At the same time, the United States has also had some successes with its approach, including in Nawa, just fifteen miles away from Marjah, where Taliban fighters have been displaced, conditions are secure, and U.S. development programs are taking hold. Such different outcomes demonstrate the highly variable character of communities—and the insurgency itself—across Afghanistan.[38]

NATO's effort to secure Kandahar, a city of great strategic and symbolic importance, has also proved difficult. Facing skeptical locals and a calculated assassination campaign by the Taliban, ISAF commanders have limited military activity inside Kandahar and have focused on outlying districts. There they have deployed additional troops, often partnered with Afghan national security forces. It is worth noting that despite heavy fighting—and some of NATO's heaviest losses of the war—Afghan civilian casualties caused by NATO went down by 30 percent over the past year. Over the same period, the Taliban's expanded use of improvised explosive devices (IEDs) increased overall civilian casualties by nearly a third.[39]

On the political front, the Obama administration's relations with President Karzai have been rocky and subject to bouts of public disagreement. They reached a low point in the fall of 2009, during and shortly after Afghanistan's deeply flawed presidential election. Karzai's visit to Washington in May 2010 focused on improving relations with the Kabul government, an effort that has carried on in subsequent senior dialogues. It is not evident that this has translated into greater trust or a more effective working partnership. The June 2010 resignations of two major cabinet officials, both considered constructive U.S. partners, raised another red flag about the political direction Kabul is headed. Over the summer, Washington sparred with Karzai over anti-corruption efforts and his decision to ban private security contractors from Afghanistan. Perhaps the most contested political issue in Afghanistan in recent months has been the reconciliation process. Distinct from the long-standing goal of reintegrating Taliban foot soldiers and junior commanders into Afghan society, reconciliation is focused on more senior Taliban members and has raised sensitive questions about what concessions the Afghan government and international community should be willing to make, what redlines they should draw, and the extent to which negotiations offer a realistic prospect for bringing the war to a close. President Karzai convened a National Consultative Peace

Jirga in June 2010 to win public endorsement for a reconciliation process, but Afghan opposition leaders—as well as regional observers with strong anti-Taliban leanings, such as India—have worried that a deal might grant too much to the Taliban.[40] Washington has declared itself open to the possibility of resolving the conflict through talks and has devoted attention to coordinating its approach with Karzai.[41] However, senior Obama administration officials have expressed varying degrees of skepticism regarding prospects for a deal.[42]

The Obama administration's fall 2009 decision to devote greater military and civilian resources to the Afghan war has been completed over the course of an extremely challenging year. Political and military setbacks have raised questions of whether the United States has the capacity to achieve its core goals with the present strategy. The following important policy challenges must be addressed in order to improve prospects for progress. If timely progress is not achieved, a more fundamental reassessment of U.S. strategy will be warranted.

- *Political weakness, corruption, and national division.* Washington needs Afghan political partners to succeed in their mission. The Afghan government remains weak. It is too often corrupt and predatory. Fundamental deficiencies of the Afghan political system divide the Afghan public and could prove fatal to U.S. efforts. Disproportionate responsibility is vested in the presidency. This imbalance is seen in the weakness of the parliament, the lack of credible political parties, and presidential control over the appointments of unelected local government officials throughout the nation. Washington should seek to build the strength of local Afghan authorities as a means to reduce public grievances against the central government but not as a means to build alternative power centers that threaten national unity.

- *Reconciliation.* The present Karzai-led reconciliation process is insufficiently representative of the wide spectrum of Afghan interests. It is raising fears among many of these groups and spurring concerns throughout the region, particularly in India. The process requires greater U.S. guidance and regional consensus building.

- *Assessing progress.* The next U.S. strategic review is slated to begin in December 2010. It should be a comprehensive assessment of whether the present strategy is working. To accomplish this goal, the Obama administration will need criteria for assessing progress, along with supporting data, or it will lose the confidence of the U.S. Congress and the American public.

– *Afghan National Security Forces.* In most instances, Afghan security forces—the army, police, and local community defense units—are not capable of taking the lead in the short term. The ANSF are being rapidly expanded at great cost, but a shortage of international trainers impedes their professionalization. Projections for future financial requirements are likely to face increasingly tough budget battles in the U.S. Congress.

– *Economic growth.* Widespread poverty and lack of infrastructure threaten self-sustaining economic development. Without greater private investment and regional economic integration, Afghanistan's vast resources, whether mineral deposits or agricultural products, will remain underutilized, and the nation will depend on international donors to support its government and people.

Policy Options and Recommendations: Pakistan

The Task Force endorses the Obama administration's effort to cultivate cooperation with Pakistan as the best way to secure vital U.S. interests in the short, medium, and long run. This approach should include significant investments in Pakistan's own stability, particularly after this summer's floods. But in order for U.S. assistance to be effective over the long term, Washington must make clear that it expects Pakistan to make a sustained effort to undermine Pakistan-based terrorist organizations and their sympathizers.

The recommendations in this chapter are intended to underscore and complement current U.S. efforts. However, the Task Force is concerned that even the best U.S. efforts in Pakistan may not succeed. Two realistic scenarios could force a fundamental reassessment of U.S. strategy and policy.

First, it is possible that Pakistan-based terrorists could conduct a large-scale attack on the United States and that the Pakistani government would—for any number of reasons—refuse to take adequate action against the perpetrators. In the aftermath of a traumatic terrorist attack, it would be impossible for U.S. leaders to accept Pakistani inaction. The United States most likely would launch a targeted strike on Pakistani territory led by Special Forces raids or aerial attacks on suspected terrorist compounds.[43] Even limited U.S. military action would provoke a strong backlash among Pakistanis. Public anger in both countries would open a rift between Washington and Islamabad.

In a second scenario, Washington could reach the conclusion that Pakistan is unwilling to improve its cooperation on U.S. counterterrorism priorities. The present U.S. policy consensus in favor of engagement with and assistance to Pakistan is largely based on the assumption that inducements, not coercion, offer the best way to win cooperation from Pakistan's people, government, and military. But this consensus requires a steady demonstration of at least incremental progress.

Frustration over Pakistan's persistent relationships with groups like LeT and the Afghan Taliban frays that consensus.[44] At some point, this frustration could cause the United States to shift its approach toward Pakistan.

In the event that fundamental strategic changes are considered, both Washington and Islamabad should have a clear understanding of the costs and benefits of alternative approaches. The most likely shift in direction for the United States would be to move from its present strategy of building a partnership through extensive outreach and inducements (carrots) to relying upon coercion and containment (sticks). Washington has a number of points of leverage with Pakistan. It could curtail civilian and military assistance. It could also work bilaterally and through international institutions, such as the International Monetary Fund (IMF) and the UN, to sanction and isolate Pakistan. U.S. operations against Pakistan-based terrorist groups could be expanded and intensified. In the region, the United States could pursue closer ties with India at Pakistan's expense.

To be clear, there are already coercive aspects to U.S. policy, but the underlying goal is to work with and through Islamabad, not against it. That would change if Washington determines that Pakistan is not prepared to take action against militant groups that threaten U.S. interests. "Sticks" would be directed against Pakistan-based terrorists, but also against the Pakistani state, in an effort to alter its policies. The U.S.-Pakistan relationship would become openly adversarial.

Americans and Pakistanis must understand that these options carry heavy risks and costs. Both sides have a great deal to lose. Containing the terrorist threat from Pakistan would be challenging if the Pakistani and U.S. governments were at odds, intelligence sharing were reduced, and U.S. officials were forced to operate from neighboring countries. NATO's presence in Afghanistan would be jeopardized without a secure logistics route through Pakistan. At the same time, Pakistan's fragile political and economic stability would be undermined by greater tensions with the United States. Pakistan's military would suffer from the loss of U.S. assistance and restricted access to training, technology, and spare parts for American-made weapons and vehicles. In general, U.S. coercion and containment of Pakistan could accelerate dangerous economic, political, and social trends inside Pakistan. Americans must recognize that as frustrating and difficult as Pakistan's situation may be today, it has the potential to get even worse.

For all of these reasons, building a more effective partnership with Pakistan is preferable. To improve the prospects for achieving core U.S. goals, the Task Force presents the following recommendations.

IMPROVE IMPLEMENTATION OF U.S. ASSISTANCE IN POST-FLOOD PAKISTAN

Washington must identify and prioritize Pakistan's most pressing needs as U.S. assistance plans are revised in the aftermath of this summer's floods. In order to make the best use of U.S. assistance for flood reconstruction and funds authorized by the Enhanced Partnership with Pakistan Act over the next five years, Washington should:

– *Meet Pakistani needs.* As Washington seeks to allocate more generous resources, it must maintain a demand-driven approach. Close collaboration is required to create and implement sustainable projects that fill gaps in Pakistan's post-flood recovery and reconstruction efforts, improve the lives of its citizens, and have supporting institutions that can put them to good use.

– *Accelerate implementation of high-profile projects.* The Task Force endorses current U.S. plans to build high-profile projects targeted at strategic sectors, such as water, power, and job creation. They should support post-flood recovery, and in this area especially, the clock is ticking to demonstrate tangible progress. Normal U.S. time lines for major development projects have the potential to frustrate Pakistanis in need. That frustration will embolden America's detractors and would be a major strategic setback. Streamlined procedures, including the hiring and development of greater United States Agency for International Development (USAID) in-house expertise, should be a priority. If implemented effectively, these sorts of projects will improve the lives of millions of Pakistanis for decades to come and can serve as a visible testament to the value of a long-term partnership with the United States.

– *Communicate U.S. intentions.* Even though past and ongoing U.S. assistance programs have been extensive, they have too often escaped Pakistani public attention. Washington should launch a sophisticated and sustained media campaign that harnesses the power of Pakistan's vibrant electronic media outlets and moves beyond standard ribbon-cuttings, official visits, and press releases.

- *Improve law and order, fight corruption.* In partnership with Pakistan's national and provincial governments, Washington should continue to fund training programs, facilities, and equipment for Pakistan's police, and should promote exchanges between U.S. and Pakistani judiciaries. These institutions are often on the front lines in fighting militancy but lack the expertise and resources needed to fulfill many of their most basic duties.

- *Build up Pakistani partners.* The interests and priorities of important sectors of Pakistan's population are fundamentally aligned with those of the United States. Members of Pakistan's business community, for instance, seek stable conditions for growth and could benefit from new U.S. initiatives to support private-sector investment. Mainstream religious leaders seek nonviolent conflict resolution. Educators, artists, and other members of civil society seek protection for speech and expression. Yet these groups tend to have little direct contact with the U.S. government. The U.S. embassy in Islamabad and consulates in Karachi, Lahore, and Peshawar should have more extensive, flexible resources at their disposal for outreach and coordination with a wide range of community leaders who often wield great influence.

- *Strengthen oversight and accountability.* To protect U.S. funds from corruption and waste, the Obama administration should implement clear and transparent monitoring mechanisms. These controls will enable greater use of Pakistani contractors. The Government Accountability Office and other U.S. government agencies should work with the Pakistani government to jointly set goals and measure annual progress. The United States and Pakistan should also create a joint oversight board that works through ministries and local governments, tracking not only inputs but also outcomes, such as job creation.

EXPAND U.S.-PAKISTAN TRADE

U.S. economic assistance can never be sufficient to meet Pakistan's enormous challenges of unemployment, poverty, and illiteracy. All of these will be made more difficult by the devastation of this summer's floods. They will be compounded over subsequent decades by rapid population growth.

Problems of such magnitude make it clear that more dramatic measures are necessary. The Obama administration should propose—and the U.S. Congress should adopt—legislation liberalizing tariffs on textile imports from Pakistan. This would help stimulate Pakistan's economy and reinforce a partnership between the American and Pakistani people. Pakistan's leaders have long sought greater access to Western markets. The United States is Pakistan's top export market. Currently, one-quarter of Pakistan's exports are bound for the United States, and one-third of foreign investment in Pakistan comes from U.S.-based investors.[45] But Pakistan still faces substantial barriers to the U.S. market.[46] Given that the textile industry accounts for 38 percent of Pakistan's industrial employment, this agreement could provide employment opportunities for millions of young Pakistanis, discouraging them from paths leading to militancy.[47] Related industries that have suffered terrible setbacks from Pakistan's floods, such as cotton farming, would also stand to benefit from the expansion of the textile sector. Consequently, the agreement would put more money in the pockets of Pakistani consumers. It is the single most effective step the United States could take to stimulate the Pakistani economy.

Relaxing U.S. textile tariffs on imports from Pakistan would not put U.S. producers at risk.[48] U.S. imports from Pakistan make up a small share (3 percent) of total U.S. imports; imports of cotton knit shirts and cotton trousers from Pakistan, for example, are 3.6 percent of total U.S. imports of those particular products.[49] Instead, a trade agreement would reshape the proportion of U.S. imports from China and other low-cost exporters that currently dominate this sector of the market.

U.S. assistance programming should be used to maximize the benefits of this agreement for regions most threatened by extremist movements. Supporting infrastructure and training projects could help shape where new textile industries are located. Pakistan's cotton-producing regions, including southern Punjab, would stand to benefit most from the deal.

Recent experience with U.S. legislation designed to facilitate greater trade and investment in Pakistan, including the Reconstruction Opportunity Zone initiative, has demonstrated the hurdles that block efforts to liberalize textile trade with Pakistan. Domestically, labor leaders, the U.S. textile industry, and members of Congress from cotton-producing regions would need reassurances that their core concerns can be met. Recognizing these challenges, the Task Force urges the Obama administration and Congress to treat this legislation as an important national security priority and a part of America's generous response to Pakistan's flood recovery effort. On a parallel track, Washington will also need a diplomatic campaign to address the inevitable objections of other textile-producing states, including China and India.

BUILD PAKISTAN'S CAPACITY TO TACKLE TERRORISM AND MILITANCY

The effectiveness of the Pakistani security services in fighting terrorism directed at others is a question of will and capacity. The United States must direct its energies to both. U.S. efforts to improve counterterror cooperation with Pakistan's military and intelligence services should continue. Washington should make clear that all violent extremist groups based in Pakistan threaten U.S., Pakistani, and regional security. There has been progress against groups that threaten the Pakistani state, but insufficient commitment against groups based in Pakistan that threaten U.S., Afghan, or Indian interests. Intelligence sharing and liaison between U.S. and Pakistani agencies is an essential component in this effort.

The Task Force recommends continued and expanded training, equipment, and facilities for police, paramilitaries, and the army. Air mobility, night vision, sniper, and surveillance capabilities all require improvement. Pakistan needs helicopters and transport aircraft to rapidly deploy its forces in remote and difficult terrain. Enhancing Pakistan's capacity for rapid and selective strikes against militant groups without alienating local communities will help it maintain security in areas so that stabilization and development efforts can take place after initial clearing operations are over. U.S. training and assistance efforts must stress the critical importance of respect for human rights and limitation of civilian casualties. U.S. defense sales and assistance should place the counterinsurgency mission first. Pakistani requests should be prioritized according to the degree to which they are appropriate to that mission.

U.S. military assistance to Pakistan should depend upon demonstrable progress toward cooperation. However, writing conditions into U.S. legislation can create severe diplomatic challenges and has, as was the case with U.S. sanctions during the 1990s, produced inflexible policies that were ultimately counterproductive. Instead, congressional leaders should work with the Obama administration to craft U.S. goals that can be shared with Pakistan through diplomatic channels. Progress along these lines should inform Washington's future decisions about assistance programming.

ACCELERATE SHIFTS IN PAKISTAN'S REGIONAL STRATEGIES

The growing ambitions and capabilities of LeT and its affiliates (and its ties to al-Qaeda) make it the ticking time bomb of South Asia. Washington should place greater pressure on Islamabad to degrade LeT's capacity and restrain its sympathizers, bearing in mind that a number of these groups enjoy widespread popular support because of their humanitarian outreach efforts. Pakistan's floods may even redound to the advantage of extremist organizations that mobilized to address local needs unmet by the state. Unlike foreign terrorist groups operating on Pakistani territory, such as al-Qaeda, LeT is entirely indigenous. Excising its tumor from Pakistan's body politic is a difficult and potentially deadly proposition that must be handled with care and precision. Washington should look for ways to support Pakistan's leaders on flood recovery efforts in parts of the country where the contest for local sympathies will be especially important to the future authority and stability of the state.

Discussion of LeT should receive priority alongside al-Qaeda and the Taliban in U.S.-Pakistan political, military, and intelligence dialogues. Tougher U.S. talk must be backed by strong evidence. The United States should therefore enhance its own intelligence and interdiction capabilities to shut down LeT's operations outside Pakistan and its recruiting activities in the United States and Europe. By sharing intelligence with India and contributing to its defensive capabilities against terrorists based in Pakistan, the United States can undercut any in Pakistan who still see strategic value in supporting militancy.

The United States should also continue its efforts against groups based in Pakistan that are trying to destabilize Afghanistan, like the

Quetta Shura Taliban and the Haqqani network. The Task Force supports the official international designation of the Haqqani network as a terrorist organization. By weakening and sanctioning these groups, the United States can demonstrate to Pakistan that they are unworthy of continued passive or active assistance. To compensate for Pakistan's apparent reluctance to attack these groups, U.S. and NATO efforts to dismantle them must remain a central component of military operations in Afghanistan and along the Pakistan border. This should include the selective use of armed drones. Rendering these groups ineffective should encourage a shift in Islamabad's approach to Afghanistan—away from armed proxies and toward constructive and legitimate political partners.

UPGRADE NUCLEAR DIALOGUE AND NONNUCLEAR ENERGY ASSISTANCE

The United States should pursue an upgraded, sustained, and forward-looking nuclear security dialogue with Pakistan that builds on prior strategic discussions and works to foster mutual trust between Washington and Islamabad. In the context of that dialogue, Washington should explore options for new confidence-building and nuclear risk–reducing measures. The dialogue should provide Washington an opportunity to raise questions about Pakistan's expanding nuclear arsenal as well as about the security of Pakistan's nuclear weapons and materials. By establishing regular contacts and enhancing the flow of information between governments, broader discussions on matters of doctrine and strategy may become possible.

The United States should not tender an unrealistic promise to Islamabad of a U.S.-Pakistan civilian nuclear agreement. It does not enjoy the support of the U.S. Congress or the international community, so prospects for passage are dim. Such a promise would only serve to frustrate both sides by raising false hopes and diverting attention from other pressing issues. But the Obama administration should do more to help tackle Pakistan's serious energy needs by nonnuclear means. Pakistan's energy crisis goes far beyond a shortage of supply: the viability of the energy sector is limited by problems of debt, ineffective regulation, corruption, theft, and inefficient distribution. The United States should work with Pakistan to address the range of institutional and policy reforms needed to attract greater private investment.

SUPPORT EFFECTIVE, DEMOCRATIC GOVERNMENT

The United States should support the democratic process and responsible civil-military relations in Pakistan. Washington should continue to engage with the broadest spectrum of Pakistani political parties without wedding itself to any one in particular. It must also recognize the limits of U.S. influence and leverage. The United States cannot rectify the civil-military power imbalance that plagues the Pakistani state. It can, however, regularly reiterate its preference for democratic rule and take pains to involve Pakistan's civilian leaders in all major bilateral dialogues. U.S. efforts to legislate specific political conditions on assistance have routinely failed to compel Pakistan's action. Instead, Washington should target support to partners and institutions that share common goals. For instance, the United States should encourage more effective governance by funneling a portion of its assistance through government ministries and local government agencies that demonstrate transparency and efficiency. This can strengthen deserving partners and show that the United States is not complicit in corruption or in siphoning U.S. aid to foreign contractors.

In areas of Pakistan where security forces have recently cleared the Taliban and other militant groups, it is particularly important for the United States to offer assistance and training for local civilian institutions. Limited administrative capacity in these areas threatens to jeopardize hard-fought military victories. Given security threats and local political sensitivities, U.S. officials may need to operate in close coordination with the Pakistani army or Frontier Corps or conduct their operations indirectly through Pakistani nationals.

ENCOURAGE INDO-PAKISTANI DIALOGUE AND TRADE

The United States should continue to encourage dialogue between India and Pakistan to reduce the chance of crisis or war. But Washington should do so quietly. Neither side will respond well to public U.S. pressure. Responsible leaders in Islamabad and New Delhi already recognize the potential benefits of a normalized relationship but face vocal, entrenched domestic opponents.

Washington should seek creative new ways to encourage Indo-Pakistani trade and investment, including U.S. technical assistance for infrastructure development along the international border and the Kashmir divide. Specifically, the United States should advance with India and Pakistan, and with multilateral institutions like the World Bank, the idea of a fund exclusively for improving the road and rail network between India and Pakistan. This would update facilities and employ large numbers of people on both sides of the border. It would demonstrate the advantages of improving bilateral relations. Over time, this effort could be expanded to power grids and gas pipelines, further demonstrating each country's stake in the economic progress of the region.

President Obama's upcoming visit to India, scheduled for November 2010, offers an important opportunity to promote this and other regional stabilization efforts.

RAISE PRIORITY OF PAKISTAN IN OTHER DIPLOMATIC DIALOGUES

China and Saudi Arabia enjoy special influence in Pakistan. They play particularly important roles in promoting a stable and growing Pakistani economy and have the capacity to deliver forceful messages on counterterrorism and other sensitive issues. Although the United States has many other priorities in its relations with these countries, the Task Force recommends that Washington elevate the discussion of Pakistan as a central issue in dialogues with Saudi and Chinese leaders.

The United States should also support multilateral efforts to coordinate policy on Pakistan. Although many sensitive political and military issues are not best addressed in multilateral settings, they can provide platforms for improving cooperation among assistance donors. Expectations should be kept firmly in check. The Friends of Democratic Pakistan group has achieved only marginal successes, frustrating officials on both sides of the table. That said, regular meetings can help to jumpstart slow bureaucratic processes and force information sharing by Pakistan and between the various donors. Washington should also seek Pakistan's membership—or at least observer status—in major international forums, such as the Group of Twenty (G20), to connect it to new power structures and familiarize it with emerging norms and responsible international behavior.

OPEN U.S. DOORS TO PAKISTANI VISITORS

One of the greatest challenges to improving relations between the people of Pakistan and the United States is the perception that America does not welcome Pakistani visitors. This perception has been reinforced by heavy-handed U.S. border security policies and clumsy implementation. For instance, after the attempted airplane attack in Detroit on Christmas Day 2009, the United States required citizens of fourteen countries, including Pakistan, to be screened separately at airports. Pakistanis widely interpreted these requirements as unfair and discriminatory, undermining U.S. efforts to cultivate a more positive image. Other miscommunications and security precautions have even disrupted official Pakistani travel within the United States. Although the U.S. government must do what is necessary to secure the borders, future decisions regarding travel restrictions and airport security should do far more to take Pakistani sensitivities, as well as the diplomatic implications of new regulations, into consideration. As a practical matter, an interagency liaison team should be established to manage and avert diplomatic incidents related to security procedures at U.S. airports.

Policy Options and Recommendations: Afghanistan

The current U.S. strategy in Afghanistan is at a critical point. To sustain American public support, the Obama administration needs to assess whether overall progress is being made, if that progress is enough to justify the costs of the present approach, and if it can be made to last. This assessment process should begin in the context of President Obama's scheduled December strategic review. The criteria for judging the core elements of the present counterinsurgency strategy should be based on answers to some critical questions, including:

– Has there been a significant improvement in the capabilities of the ANSF?

– Is momentum shifting against the insurgency in contested areas?

– Once NATO operations have taken place, is normal life starting to return?

– Is progress being made in building local security and civilian capabilities?

– Has the government in Kabul taken serious steps to combat corruption?

As this assessment unfolds, the Obama administration should share with Congress its answers to these questions, along with extensive supporting data. No single measure will define progress. The president has said that the United States will continue its present military surge until July 2011. If progress is being made, the United States should be able to draw down its forces starting in July 2011, based on conditions on the ground. However, if U.S. efforts are not working, a more significant drawdown to a narrower mission that emphasizes counterterror objectives with fewer U.S. forces will be warranted. As the war moves into its tenth year, opposition has grown. Critics of the U.S. military surge and counterinsurgency effort question the strategy, its execution, and whether it can succeed. They believe that the American public will not bear the costs of war in Afghanistan much longer; that the Afghan state will remain predatory and corrupt, its nascent security forces dependent on foreign troops; and that the range of security threats now facing Afghanistan makes the war unwinnable. They put forth a range of strategic alternatives to the present U.S. counterinsurgency campaign. None of them is without its own significant risks and costs.

An alternative to the present U.S. strategy calls for the United States to address the threat of international terrorism in Afghanistan with a military and civilian posture that is significantly smaller, more affordable, and less vulnerable.[50] A "light footprint,"—some argue as few as ten thousand to twenty thousand troops—led by Special Operations Forces armed with cash, weapons, surveillance, and the ability to call in U.S. airpower, could partner with elements of the Afghan state and nonstate power brokers to continue counterterror missions long after the bulk of NATO forces have pulled out. Even if the Kabul government is unable to retain control over large portions of its territory, a force of this sort would attempt to prop up enough partners to retain sufficient bases inside Afghanistan. Washington would also continue to partner with Islamabad on the other side of the border. A smaller military force would be less reliant upon Pakistani supply lines, creating an added benefit of reducing Islamabad's leverage over U.S. operations.

By demonstrating that the United States is primarily concerned with combating international terrorists, Washington might find new opportunities to negotiate with some members of the Afghan Taliban, cleaving them from al-Qaeda and other terrorist groups with more extreme global ambitions. The reduced NATO commitment to Afghanistan could lead states like China, Iran, and Russia—which contribute little to security efforts and pursue self-serving agendas—to think more seriously about issues of regional security. It might spark a new round of regional diplomacy with the potential to create a messy but workable Afghan peace settlement. As for shoring up Pakistan's stability, U.S. forces could try to assist Islamabad against militant threats that emerge on the Afghan side of the border while Washington continues to work against other Pakistan-based terrorist networks, like LeT.

All of these scenarios are conceivable, but they hinge on optimistic assumptions. A shift to a light-footprint approach would carry significant risks. A narrow counterterror campaign would almost certainly

offer Americans less protection against international terrorism than
the present strategy.[51] This is because U.S. Special Forces would be
operating in a deteriorating security environment with even fewer sympathetic Afghan partners. They would find it harder to move around
the country to collect intelligence or to attack the enemy. With fewer
personnel or facilities for training, U.S. forces would face greater challenges in building capable Afghan troops or local security units.

A light footprint would also have difficulty dealing with the fact that
in recent years al-Qaeda has forged closer ties with elements of the
Afghan Taliban, especially the Haqqani network. This new generation
of Taliban fighters is more likely to share al-Qaeda's vision of global
jihad. It is plausible that the Taliban would revert to past practices,
expanding its partnership with international terrorists as a means to
destroy Afghan opponents. If successful, this would make it even harder
for the United States to find willing and capable Afghan partners.

Under those circumstances, Afghanistan could easily fracture into
full-fledged civil war. That war would be every bit as devastating as
earlier Afghan conflicts, creating millions of refugees and widespread
humanitarian tragedy. By its decision to remain focused on a narrow
counterterror mission, the United States would be held partly to blame
for the suffering, making many Afghans even less willing to assist U.S.
operations. A light footprint would bring Afghanistan no closer to
enduring political or economic stability. It would offer little in the way
of a realistic plan for a full, responsible U.S. military withdrawal. The
United States could find itself trapped in a long, bloody quagmire, with
worse prospects than it faces today.

The Task Force finds that if Afghanistan falls back into civil war,
its neighbors are more likely to take sides than to stand apart or try
to dampen the conflict. The Indo-Pakistani competition in Afghanistan could be particularly fierce and would hurt their broader bilateral
relationship. The United States would almost certainly find itself at
odds with Pakistan's choice of proxy forces in Afghanistan—the Taliban and its affiliates. Those differences would exacerbate tensions
that already exist between Islamabad and Washington. All of these
dynamics would take an added toll on the overstressed Pakistani state
and endanger its stability.

Based on these short-term threats and long-term costs, the Task
Force judges that the light-footprint alternative poses significant risks
to U.S. interests. Even so, the United States should consider alternatives

of this sort if it judges that timely, demonstrable progress is not being made with the current approach. Either way, Washington must take urgent steps to address the serious, unmet challenges with the present approach that skeptics have identified. Three stand out. First, the United States needs to find and strengthen Afghan political partners capable of playing constructive roles in the counterinsurgency effort. Second, it needs to gain confidence that Afghan security forces can begin to assume responsibility for security at an acceptable cost. Third, it needs to identify the economic means by which Afghanistan can sustain its people and government, offering opportunities other than violence and illicit activity.

The Task Force recommends the following steps for U.S. strategy and policy in order to better address these challenges.

SEIZE THE POLITICAL INITIATIVE

The solution to Afghanistan's insurgency will need to be political, not military. Irreconcilable insurgents will need to be killed or captured, but enduring stability will come only when the vast majority of Afghanistan's people reach minimally acceptable terms with their state. That political arrangement, backed by more capable Afghan security forces, economic development, and regional diplomacy, offers the United States the best way to achieve a permanent withdrawal from Afghanistan at a reduced risk of resurgent terrorism or civil war.

The precise form of Afghanistan's political arrangement is less important than the requirement that its government should not be a contributor to public discontent, insecurity, and division. Ineffective, corrupt, at times predatory, the Afghan state now bears some responsibility for the Taliban insurgency. The United States should continue to seek leverage with the Karzai government, using everything from targeted coercion to assistance incentives, to improve its record on corruption, to appoint more capable officials at the national and local levels, and to take ownership of important components of the counterinsurgency mission.

Yet the problem is bigger than Karzai, his allies, or his appointees. The 2009 presidential elections exposed flaws in the Afghan political system and exacerbated rifts among major Afghan leaders. Natural U.S. partners—in Afghanistan's parliament, business community, and civil society—have been alienated by Washington's heavy investment in the presidency. Karzai's newly initiated reconciliation process has so far failed to create more than the illusion of national consensus. The regional coalition that supported the post-Taliban process of building a new Afghan state has also fallen into disrepair. In response, the United States needs an approach that combines three major initiatives: political reform, national reconciliation, and regional diplomacy.

U.S. officials should encourage political reform that will allow for greater power sharing and accountability while encouraging national unity. Effective reforms could come in many shapes and sizes. Amendments to the electoral laws, for instance, could enable political parties and help to strengthen the Afghan parliament. Reforms to the appointment process for governors, police chiefs, and so on could make these officeholders more directly accountable to local communities.

Karzai and other beneficiaries of the current system will oppose such changes, but these individuals are not immune to domestic or international pressure. Washington should identify several high-priority reform initiatives, then seize chances for leverage and influence as they arise. In this effort, the United States can harness popular discontent rather than—as is often the case—suffer from association with the status quo. Eager and capable Afghan political partners would be quick to join a U.S.-led reform effort if it is clear that Washington is serious about change.

The national reconciliation process also offers a potential opening for constitutional reform. Insurgent leaders have explicitly rejected the present constitution and are unlikely to reenter Afghan politics without certain amendments. The two political initiatives—reform and reconciliation—should therefore be managed in tandem. Washington should seek an inclusive negotiation process that—unlike the present mechanism—involves a wide range of groups beyond President Karzai's inner circle. By bringing more Afghan interests to the table, the United States is also more likely to see its own core interests served, such as making sure that insurgents make a clear break with al-Qaeda. The process is unlikely to yield any rapid breakthroughs, but it should be a part of Washington's broader approach. Through various means, including negotiation, most of today's Afghan insurgents must eventually be brought back into Afghanistan's political, social, and economic mainstream.

As any Afghan reconciliation process unfolds, the United States should work to leverage the interests of regional powers in ways that can support a stable settlement. No deal will endure that does not satisfy bedrock regional interests. Pakistan will have a particularly important role to play, but Washington should also move quickly to enlist the participation of India, China, the Arab Gulf states, Russia, and the Central Asian republics. Iran must be at the table as well. A small contact group would offer the best mechanism for hammering out a regional agreement on basic terms for an Afghan settlement.

REALISTIC EXPANSION OF AFGHAN SECURITY FORCES

The ANSF are a central pillar in the Obama administration's exit strategy for Afghanistan. Over time, they—along with local community defense units—must assume a greater security responsibility in order for U.S. and other coalition forces to withdraw. But NATO need not build an Afghan army in its image. The primary mission of the ANSF should be to support NATO-led operations, to maintain security after insurgents have been cleared, and ultimately to provide security to the population. Such missions may be challenging, but they do not require the creation of a military capable of full-spectrum operations. As it builds the Afghan army, NATO should therefore continue to devote its main resources to building light infantry forces. It is not clear, for instance, that current plans to fund fixed-wing aircraft and training for the Afghan National Army Air Corps are critical to the most urgent missions at hand.[52] Bearing more limited expectations in mind, the goal of rapid ANSF expansion to bolster population security becomes more conceivable, if still extremely difficult.

The United States is devoting unprecedented resources to ANSF expansion, with budgets that may be difficult for the U.S. Congress to accept over time and that will be too large for the Kabul government to foot on its own. As of 2008, the Afghan government could provide only $320 million toward the annual cost of the ANSF, a figure recently projected at $6 billion to $7 billion.[53] Even a considerably reduced security assistance program will therefore require strong, consistent support from the international community for the foreseeable future. Greater commitments from allies and the private sector could help reduce long-term costs to the United States. In particular, the UN-administered Law and Order Trust Fund, which provides salaries, equipment, and other support to Afghanistan's police, should be expanded.[54]

Despite massive U.S. expenditures and the clear strategic priority of the ANSF, hundreds of additional trainers are needed to adequately staff NATO's ANSF training mission. Washington should press its allies and partners to rapidly fulfill their pledges of institutional and embedded trainers and mentors for the ANA and Afghan National Police (ANP).

Recruitment and training for the ANP, a force essential to a population-centric counterinsurgency strategy, has lagged years behind that of the army. The ANP should blend community policing, paramilitary skills, and investigative capabilities. To increase professionalism and reduce corruption, mentoring and partnering with police trainers is needed at the local level. The best trainers have appropriate professional experience; regular military units are not well suited to the task. A public education campaign designed to inform Afghans about the proper role of the police and ways that the public can report abusive predatory practices would also help to accelerate the ANP reform process.

New opportunities for fielding Afghan security forces should be considered. NATO's recent initiatives to expand community defense forces have merit. Although the fighting potential of community policing forces is not yet clear, and there will undoubtedly be abuses of the system, the threat that these groups might pose to Kabul's authority pales in comparison with the immediate need to oppose Taliban advances and build public security. To establish the ultimate legal and political authority of the Afghan government, these forces have appropriately been placed under the auspices of the Afghan interior ministry.

PROMOTE PRIVATE SECTOR
ECONOMIC GROWTH

International assistance for Afghanistan has played a tangible and positive role in the lives of millions. In partnership with other donors, USAID successfully led an effort that increased the percentage of Afghans with access to some form of health care from 9 percent in 2002 to more than 85 percent in 2010. To facilitate the means of communication and transportation for Afghans, the agency rehabilitated over 1,677 kilometers of roads and worked to establish four mobile companies that serve 6.5 million subscribers.[55]

That said, there is more that can be done to create economic growth that is sustainable and offers opportunities for the many Afghans who are locked into the war economy or narcotics trade. One of the primary purposes of U.S. assistance should be to improve conditions for private investment and regional trade. Diplomatic outreach to China, India, and other potential investors should stress their central importance to Afghanistan's stability as well as the realistic potential for profit. Unless Afghan and international businesspeople take a long-term interest in Afghanistan, Kabul will never expand its revenue stream, and there will never be enough jobs for ex-militia members. In that case, whatever near-term stability the surge might deliver would soon be washed away by renewed violence.

The following policy recommendations are intended to help enable sustainable Afghan economic growth, recognizing that there will be no quick fixes to the problems at hand:

– *Leverage extractive industries.* Recent surveys estimate that the market value of Afghan natural resources could run into the trillions of U.S. dollars.[56] Afghanistan would benefit from technical and planning assistance as it navigates the high-stakes process of contracting with foreign governments and firms as well as making sensitive political decisions about how to allocate revenues. Washington should support continued Afghan participation in the Extractive Industries Transparency Initiative as a means to avoid the worst abuses—corruption, bribery, etc.—often associated with major natural resource discoveries.[57]

– *Accelerate regional trade and transit.* Security threats and political tensions obstruct trade and transit throughout the region. Pakistani and Afghan economic prospects over the medium to long run, however, will depend largely on their ability to connect to regional markets. Capitalizing on Afghanistan's position at the crossroads of land trade routes could provide the country with substantial customs revenues. Opening pathways to major regional importers could vastly expand business opportunities for Afghanistan's exporters. The United States should help lay the groundwork for future economic integration by creating incentives for regional investment and trade corridors in and through Afghanistan. Washington should throw its weight behind initiatives that aim to increase cross-border trade through infrastructure projects, such as expressways and rail links.[58] The United States should also work with Kabul and Islamabad to ensure the rapid implementation of the recent Afghanistan-Pakistan Transit Trade Agreement, which should permit Afghan produce to be trucked across Pakistan to buyers in India.

— *Buy Afghan.* As the international coalition spends billions of dollars to sustain its operations in Afghanistan, every opportunity should be explored to procure goods from Afghan businesses, subject to safeguards against corruption and abuse. Every dollar spent will then do double duty, first providing necessary goods and services, and then helping to develop the Afghan private sector.

Conclusion

The Task Force endorses strategies for Pakistan and Afghanistan that place severe demands on the American people. Tens of thousands of U.S. forces are already engaged in bloody, exhausting combat; thousands of U.S. civilians in the region labor under difficult, unfamiliar conditions; and billions of American taxpayer dollars flow into the region each month. The Task Force does so knowing that, at best, the margin for U.S. victory is likely to be slim. And it does so in a time-bound way: if President Obama's December strategic review shows that progress is not being made, the United States should move quickly to recalculate its military presence in Afghanistan.

The United States faces real dangers in Pakistan and Afghanistan that demand considerable attention, no matter what strategy Washington implements. An insurgency laced with international terrorism is a menacing threat to regional and global security. Nuclear-armed Pakistan's persistent ties to some of these groups, particularly LeT and elements of the Afghan Taliban, obstruct closer American cooperation and undermine the long-term stability of the world's second-largest Muslim-majority state.

Afghanistan's instability could drag the region into a proxy war that would place still greater stresses on Pakistan, weaken fragile, energy-rich Central Asian states, and exacerbate tensions between New Delhi and Islamabad. The Task Force takes seriously the possibility that a rapid U.S. exit from an unstable Afghanistan could re-create safe havens for international terrorism.

In Pakistan, if dangerous social, political, and economic trends are not tackled now, they will tax the world's security and collective resources for generations to come. In a worst-case scenario, a radicalized, nuclear-armed Pakistan of three hundred million people in 2050 would be an almost unimaginable threat to global order.

At present, the United States aims to address these threats by building partnerships with Pakistani and Afghan allies that will turn the heavy investments of today into sustainable, less costly, more solid options over the long haul. These partnerships are essential. Without them, the United States will not achieve its objectives. In fighting terrorism and insurgency, progress should be measured by what America builds, not just by whom it captures or kills. Improved cooperation with Pakistan, strengthened Afghan security forces, and more territory secured from Taliban control constitute successes along the way. Political reforms and economic development efforts must follow in order for the region to achieve enduring stability. A final U.S. victory in the region will not come through an enemy's formal surrender; it will come when U.S. partners in Pakistan and Afghanistan are committed and stable enough to secure their own territories and U.S. forces can withdraw completely.

The Task Force is well aware of the tough fiscal trade-offs between struggles abroad and priorities at home. The present U.S. strategy places pressure on U.S. budgets at precisely the same time as American and global economic circumstances are forcing other painful compromises. The budgetary gymnastics required to advance the Task Force's preferred approach to Afghanistan and Pakistan cannot be overlooked. It is undeniable, for instance, that delivering $1.5 billion per year in civilian assistance to Pakistan, sustaining troops in Afghanistan at $6 billion to $7 billion per year, and building the in-house capacity of USAID to formulate, implement, and monitor programs in Afghanistan will come at a cost to other domestic projects. This is why it is essential to determine whether the present effort is making progress in a timely way. If not, less expensive options must be considered.

Budget-conscious Americans should not, however, equate U.S. assistance programming in Pakistan and Afghanistan—for projects like roads, schools, or irrigation canals—with charity. It is done with a strategic, as well as a humanitarian, purpose: to help build more stable and more secure societies that are less likely to export violence and extremism. The effort to open the U.S. market to greater textile imports from Pakistan will raise opposition from U.S. labor groups and textile producers, even if—as preliminary studies indicate—neither one would actually suffer from the deal. Overcoming political obstacles will require energy and persistence. To have any hope of success, the Obama administration must view its coordination with Congress as an essential component of its overseas mission.

Without strong U.S. leadership, others have shown themselves unwilling or unable to confront the challenges posed by Pakistan or Afghanistan. The region has historically demonstrated a great proclivity for competition and war. Too many of the world's powerful states would prefer to look the other way rather than shoulder a greater responsibility. For now, the United States should assume the lead, with the goal of encouraging and enabling its Pakistani and Afghan partners to build a more secure future. Yet even the United States cannot afford to continue down this costly path unless the potential for enduring progress remains in sight. After nine years of U.S. war in the region, time and patience are understandably short.

Additional or Dissenting Views

The report makes clear that any early and substantial reduction in the American commitment to Afghanistan will increase the risks to the United States, including the risk of terrorist attacks originating from there. It goes on, however, to recommend a reduction in that commitment beginning next summer, whether or not current efforts to counter the Taliban insurgency are making progress. We cannot concur in prejudging what the president should decide if he concludes in 2011 that our current strategy is not working. The global and regional context for any decision in mid-2011 simply cannot be foreseen nine months in advance. While lack of progress by July 2011 should rightfully be seen as a dangerous indicator, the most logical response is to reassess the strategy—not to reflexively end it and move to large-scale withdrawal. Determining that response now in the absence of the broader national security context of summer 2011 is an unsound recommendation that would preemptively tie the president's hands.

David W. Barno, Joseph J. Collins, James F. Dobbins, John A. Gastright, John M. Keane, John A. Nagl, John D. Negroponte, Ashley J. Tellis

On pages 5, 13, and 56, the report suggests that if current efforts do not work, in July 2011 "a drawdown to a narrower military mission would be warranted" (page 5). In my view, if the current strategy falters, an amended full-service counterinsurgency effort should be tried first, before falling back on a narrower approach. We should not harness U.S. national interests in a protracted conflict to a self-imposed deadline. In any case, whether a broad or narrower mission follows in July 2011, training and advising Afghan national security forces are more critical to the outcome of this conflict than any form of counterterrorism

or development policy are. Robust Afghan national security forces—
police and military—are the key to our exit strategy.

Joseph J. Collins

While I generally concur with the analysis, I do not agree with many of
the recommendations, particularly with regards to Afghanistan.

C. Christine Fair

The Task Force report is a highly insightful and useful document, but
is not incisive enough in assessing current prospects for success in
Afghanistan or in prescribing a viable alternative strategy.

The report provides scant hope that our current strategy can succeed, yet recommends we continue until July 2011. It catalogues the many
risks associated with an alternative "light-footprint" strategy, strongly
suggesting that it, too, cannot succeed, but it suggests it be attempted
anyway. One might thus conclude that the U.S. situation in Afghanistan
is hopeless, and that the United States should withdraw; the report does
not say this either.

I believe the current U.S. strategy cannot, in fact, succeed: the force
posture it requires is politically unsustainable beyond next summer, and
such progress as might be generated by then cannot be sustained by the
Afghan central government in contested areas. The time to adopt a sustainable strategy is now; if we employ means that conform to Afghan
realities, the situation will be far from hopeless.

The report suggests that in opting for a light-footprint strategy, the
United States would be choosing "managing terrorist threats" over
"investing in sustainable Afghan options." On the contrary, I believe
that a patient, limited U.S. effort that balances development of a sustain-
ably small but capable Afghan army with sponsorship and mentoring
of local militia forces tied to authentic, locally accountable leaders—
sometimes disparaged as "warlords"—can provide gradual and sustainable progress in countering the Taliban while providing a platform for
U.S.-led counterterror operations.

Robert L. Grenier

I do not share this report's analysis and recommendations in every respect. In particular, I believe that the report's suggestion that Washington has a credible, coercive fall-back position to convince Pakistan's security managers to change course is misplaced. In past crises, when the possibilities of leveraging unwelcome choices on Pakistan's decision-makers were far better than at present, and when faced with far more concerted, top-down U.S. pressures, Pakistan's leaders successfully parried Washington's pressures to take actions that were perceived to be unacceptable on national security or domestic political grounds. This track record, as reflected in Pakistan's pursuit of nuclear weapon capabilities, its protection of unconventional military options to influence Afghanistan's future, and its policies to keep India off-balance, provides a cautionary tale of Washington's ability to successfully manipulate carrots and sticks.

To hold out the expectation that, this time around, with such a heavy U.S. military presence in Afghanistan dependent on Pakistani logistical support, Washington can coercively manipulate Pakistan's orientation toward the Lashkar-e-Taiba, the Afghan Taliban, Kabul, and New Delhi, seems unwise. Pakistan's security managers have to come to their own realization that their policies have resulted in profound damage to their country. If they do not, the natural result, with no U.S. manipulation necessary, will be the continued mortgaging of Pakistan's future, its distancing from the West, and its economic decline. Likewise, it is hard for me to envision an enduring, positive outcome in Afghanistan without suitable authorities to whom U.S. forces can hand over their gains.

Michael Krepon

I agree with the recommendations of this report, but two issues deserve more prominence.

First, the United States and Pakistan have a major difference in priorities and objectives in Afghanistan. Pakistani leaders' real objective is to eliminate Indian influence in Afghanistan, and they are convinced that the U.S. military aims to depart as quickly as possible. As a result, Pakistan wants to make Afghanistan as close as possible to a client state, regardless of whether that state respects U.S. concerns about extra-regional terrorism.

The report rightly recommends that the United States build up Afghan state institutions. The United States should also hem in extremist organizations linked to the Pakistan army and form a regional consultative mechanism that includes Afghanistan's neighbors, including Iran and India, to facilitate stability.

Second, the role of the private sector in Pakistan's development deserves greater priority both in the report and in U.S. policy. Kerry-Lugar-Berman provides generous funding, some of which ought to be used to facilitate start-up companies and help forge links with U.S. business. Private business initiatives in Afghanistan would be more powerful if combined with the expansion of trade and transit links between Pakistan and India, something the United States could discreetly encourage.

Teresita C. Schaffer

Endnotes

1. Ian S. Livingston and Michael O'Hanlon, *Pakistan Index*, Brookings Institution, August 31, 2010.
2. Washington reimbursed Pakistan $756 million in FY 2010 for operations related to the war in Afghanistan. U.S. assistance figures are found in K. Alan Kronstadt, "Pakistan: Key Current Issues and Developments," *Congressional Research Service Report for Congress*, R41307, June 1, 2010, p. 67.
3. Joby Warrick and Peter Finn, "CIA director says secret attacks in Pakistan have hobbled al-Qaeda," *Washington Post*, March 18, 2010; Greg Miller, "CIA says gets money's worth from Pakistani ISI," *Los Angeles Times*, November 15, 2009. For a list of many of the top al-Qaeda leaders killed or captured by Pakistan forces, see http://www.alertnet.org/thenews/newsdesk/L01675883.htm.
4. For example, in January 2010, charges were filed against Chicago-based U.S. citizen David Coleman Headley and Canadian citizen Tahawwur Rana for conspiring with LeT to plan a terrorist attack against a Danish newspaper as well as the November 2008 terrorist attacks in Mumbai—which killed approximately 164 people, including six Americans. Headley attended several LeT training camps beginning in 2003. He pleaded guilty to a dozen federal terrorism charges, including charges involving the Mumbai and Denmark plots, in March 2010. Details of the plea are outlined in a U.S. Justice Department Office of Public Affairs press release dated March 18, 2010, http://www.justice.gov/opa/pr/2010/March/10-ag-277.html.
5. Dennis C. Blair, "Annual Threat Assessment of the U.S. Intelligence Community," Senate Select Committee on Intelligence, February 2, 2010, p. 11.
6. Livingston and O'Hanlon, *Pakistan Index*.
7. Phil Stewart, "Pakistan's Army accused of extra-judicial killings," *Reuters*, April 5, 2010.
8. Transparency International, for example, ranked Pakistan 139 out of 180 countries in its 2009 study of perceptions of government corruption.
9. Based on estimated population growth of five million per year. See Toufiq Siddiqi, "Pakistan, Afghanistan, and the U.S.: Shared Concerns and Concerted Responses," East-West Center, 2010, http://www.eastwestcenter.org/news-center/east-west-wire/pakistan-afghanistan-and-the-us-shared-concerns-and-concerted-responses/.
10. "Pakistan Is Rapidly Adding Nuclear Arms, U.S. Says," *New York Times*, May 17, 2009.
11. "1388 National Budget," Ministry of Finance, Islamic Republic of Afghanistan, 2009.
12. William H. McMichael, "Afghan army improves, but still lacks leaders," *Marine Corps Times*, June 3, 2010.
13. Jim Michaels, "Afghan troops reach 240,000 goal early," *USA Today*, August 11, 2010.
14. Alissa J. Rubin, "Afghans to Form Local Forces to Fight Taliban," *New York Times*, July 14, 2010, A1.
15. For a recent history that makes this point, see Thomas Barfield, *Afghanistan: A Cultural and Political History* (Princeton, NJ: Princeton University Press, 2010).

16. James Risen, "U.S. Identifies Vast Mineral Riches in Afghanistan," *New York Times*, June 13, 2010, A1.

17. Michael Wines, "China Willing to Spend Big on Afghan Commerce," *New York Times*, December 30, 2009, A1.

18. Karen DeYoung, "U.S. hopes Afghanistan-Pakistan trade deal boosts cooperation in war effort," *Washington Post*, July 19, 2010.

19. The U.S.-led coalition in Afghanistan has relied heavily on Pakistani cooperation in transporting supplies to the theater. Currently, Pakistan serves as a thoroughfare for over 80 percent of container cargo and 40 percent of fuel bound for Afghanistan. Michael O'Hanlon et al., *Pakistan Index*, Brookings Institution, 2010.

20. See Public Law 111-73, Enhanced Partnership with Pakistan Act of 2009 (signed into law October 15, 2009), http://frwebgate.access.gpo.gov/cgi-bin/getdoc.cgi?dbname=111_cong_public_laws&docid=f:publ073.111.pdf.

21. Hearing to Receive Testimony on the Challenges Facing the Department of Defense, U.S. Senate Committee on Armed Committee, January 27, 2009, http://armed-services.senate.gov/Transcripts/2009/01%20January/A%20Full%20Committee/09-02%20-%201-27-09.pdf.

22. Dexter Filkins, *The Forever War* (New York: Knopf, 2008).

23. Hillary Clinton, "Opening Remarks at U.S.-Pakistan Strategic Dialogue," July 19, 2010, http://www.state.gov/secretary/rm/2010/07/144827.htm.

24. Information on flood response from U.S. Department of State website, http://www.state.gov/r/pa/prs/ps/2010/08/146107.htm.

25. Glenn Kessler, "Washington objects to China-Pakistan nuclear deal," *Washington Post*, June 14, 2010.

26. This includes payments through the Coalition Support Fund. See K. Alan Kronstadt, "Direct Overt U.S. Aid and Military Reimbursements to Pakistan, FY2002–FY2011," Congressional Research Service, June 7, 2010, http://www.fas.org/sgp/crs/row/pakaid.pdf. See also Griff Witte, "Billions of Aid Dollars Buy U.S. Little Goodwill in Pakistan," *Washington Post*, August 24, 2010.

27. For details, see K. Alan Kronstadt, "Major U.S. Arms Sales and Grants to Pakistan since 2001," Congressional Research Service, March 23, 2010, http://www.fas.org/sgp/crs/row/pakarms.pdf.

28. Peter Bergen and Katherine Tiedemann, "The Year of the Drone: An Analysis of U.S. Drone Strikes in Pakistan, 2004–2010," New America Foundation, February 24, 2010, http://www.humansecuritygateway.com/documents/NAF_YearOfTheDrone.pdf.

29. Ibid.

30. For example, the U.S. tariff rate on Chinese exports is 3 percent, versus 10 percent on Pakistani exports. The United States raises the same tariff revenue from Pakistan's $3.7 billion in exports as from France's $37 billion in textile exports. See U.S.-Pakistan Business Council, "Strengthening the U.S.-Pakistan Economic Partnership," http://www.uschamber.com/publications/reports/0903_uspakistan.htm; Pakistan Policy Working Group, "The Next Chapter," http://www.brookings.edu/~/media/Files/rc/reports/2008/09_pakistan_cohen/09_pakistan_cohen.pdf. On the size of the Pakistani textile industry, see Aftab A. Khan and Mehreen Khan, "Pakistan Textile Industry Facing New Challenges," *Research Journal of International Studies*, Issue 14, May 2010, http://www.eurojournals.com/rjis_14_04.pdf.

31. "Special Operations Triple in Afghanistan—McChrystal," *New York Times*, June 10, 2010, http://www.nytimes.com/reuters/2010/06/10/world/international-uk-afghanistan-usa-forces.html?ref=world.

32. Curt Tarnoff, "Afghanistan: U.S. Foreign Assistance," R40699 (Washington, DC: Congressional Research Service, March 5, 2010), pp. 10–11, http://fpc.state.gov/documents/organization/139236.pdf; NATO Training Mission-Afghanistan Command Update,

briefing to Task Force, Kabul, February 2010.

33. Alissa J. Rubin, "Afghans to Form Local Forces to Fight Taliban," *New York Times,* July 14, 2010, A1.

34. U.S. Department of Defense, *Report on Progress toward Security and Stability in Afghanistan* (Washington, DC: Government Printing Office, April 2010), p. 9, http://www.defense.gov/pubs/pdfs/Report_Final_SecDef_04_26_10.pdf.

35. Office of the Special Representative for Afghanistan and Pakistan, "Afghanistan and Pakistan Regional Stabilization Strategy," U.S. Department of State, February 2010, pp. 16–17, http://www.state.gov/documents/organization/135728.pdf; Senate Foreign Relations Committee, "Afghanistan's Narco War: Breaking the Link between Drug Traffickers and Insurgents," 111th Cong., 1st sess., 2009, Committee Print 29, August 10, 2009, http://frwebgate.access.gpo.gov/cgi-bin/getdoc.cgi?dbname=111_cong_senate_committee_prints&docid=f:51521.pdf.

36. The White House, "Remarks by the President in Address to the Nation on the Way Forward in Afghanistan and Pakistan," U.S. Military Academy at West Point, December 1, 2009, http://www.whitehouse.gov/the-press-office/remarks-president-address-nation-way-forward-afghanistan-and-pakistan.

37. Kabul International Conference on Afghanistan Communiqué, July 20, 2010, http://graphics8.nytimes.com/packages/pdf/world/2010/Kabul-Conference-Communique.pdf.

38. This point is made quite effectively by Rajiv Chandrasekaran, "Two Afghan towns. One success story," *Washington Post,* July 25, 2010.

39. Jan Boone, "Afghanistan Civilian Deaths up 31% this Year, Says United Nations," *Guardian,* August 10, 2010.

40. Joshua Partlow, "Minority leaders leaving Karzai's side over leader's overtures to insurgents," *Washington Post,* July 23, 2010.

41. White House, "Joint Statement from the President and President Karzai of Afghanistan," May 12, 2010, http://www.whitehouse.gov/the-press-office/joint-statement-president-and-president-karzai-afghanistan.

42. Mark Landler and Thom Shanker, "U.S. May Label Pakistan Militants as Terrorists," *New York Times,* July 13, 2010.

43. See Greg Miller, "Options studied for a possible Pakistan strike," *Washington Post,* May 29, 2010, http://www.washingtonpost.com/wp-dyn/content/article/2010/05/28/AR2010052804854.html.

44. This is one of the most important potential implications of the WikiLeak online publication of intelligence documents related to the war in Afghanistan. See Mark Mazzetti, Jane Perlez, Eric Schmitt, and Andrew W. Lehren, "Pakistan Aids Insurgency in Afghanistan, Reports Assert," *New York Times,* July 25, 2010.

45. K. Alan Kronstadt, *Pakistan-U.S. Relations,* RL33498 (Washington, DC: Congressional Research Service, February 2009), http://www.fas.org/sgp/crs/row/RL33498.pdf.

46. Ibid., p. 83.

47. Khan and Khan, "Pakistan Textile Industry Facing New Challenges."

48. Mary Jane Bolle, "Afghanistan and Pakistan Reconstruction Opportunity Zones: Issues and Arguments," R40627 (Washington, DC: Congressional Research Service, October 15, 2009), p. 14, http://www.fas.org/sgp/crs/row/R40627.pdf.

49. "Extending duty-free, quota-free market access for all exports from UN-designated least developed countries (LDCs), plus other low-income countries, including Pakistan and Vietnam, would reduce U.S. textile production by less than 1% and apparel production by only 0.1%. About half that impact is due to increased imports from LDCs, and the remainder is due mostly to higher imports from Vietnam, whose exports of textiles and apparel were nearly twice those of Pakistan in 2008." Kimberly

Ann Elliot, "Stimulating Pakistani Exports and Job Creation," Center for Global Development, April 2010, p. 2, http://www.cgdev.org/files/1424056_file_Elliott_Pakistan_Trade_Preference.pdf.

50. Variations on this line of reasoning include Richard Haass, "We're Not Winning. It's Not Worth It," *Newsweek*, July 18, 2010; Austin Long, "Small Is Beautiful: The Counterterrorism Option in Afghanistan, *Orbis*, Spring 2010, pp. 199–214; and Robert Blackwill, "A De Facto Partition for Afghanistan," *Politico*, July 7, 2010.

51. John F. Burns, "McChrystal Rejects Scaling Down Afghan Military Aims," *New York Times*, October 1, 2009.

52. Fixed-wing trainers and close air support aircraft comprise roughly $250 million of the FY 2010 request (including the supplemental). For a full breakdown of the Afghan Security Forces Fund, see "Justification for FY 2010 Supplemental Afghanistan Security Forces Fund (ASFF)," Office of the Secretary of Defense, February 2010, http://asafm.army.mil/Documents/OfficeDocuments/Budget/BudgetMaterials/FY11/OCO//asff-sup.pdf.

53. Steve Bowman and Catherine Dale, "War in Afghanistan: Strategy, Military Operations, and Issues for Congress," Congressional Research Service, June 8, 2010, http://www.fas.org/sgp/crs/natsec/R40156.pdf.

54. For more information, see United Nations Development Programme, "Law and Order Trust Fund for Afghanistan (LOTFA)—Phase V: Annual Progress Report 2009," http://www.undp.org.af/Projects/2009AnnualReports/LOTFAV_APR09.pdf.

55. United States Agency for International Development, "Afghanistan," July 27, 2010, http://www.usaid.gov/locations/asia/countries/afghanistan/.

56. These estimates are generated, in part, by projecting future market values of untapped Afghan mineral and energy deposits identified by the U.S. Geological Survey. See http://afghanistan.cr.usgs.gov/airborne.php.

57. See Paul Collier, "In Afghanistan, a Threat of Plunder," *New York Times*, July 19, 2010.

58. One example of this initiative is found in S. Frederick Starr and Andrew C. Kutchins, "The Key to Success in Afghanistan: A Modern Silk Road Strategy," Central Asia-Caucasus Institute Silk Road Studies Program, May 2010, at http://www.silkroadstudies.org/new/docs/silkroadpapers/1005Afghan.pdf.

Task Force Members

Task Force members are asked to join a consensus signifying that they endorse "the general policy thrust and judgments reached by the group, though not necessarily every finding and recommendation." They participate in the Task Force in their individual, not their institutional, capacities.

Richard L. Armitage is the president of Armitage International and a former deputy secretary of state (2001–2005). Prior to returning to government service in 2001, Armitage was president of Armitage Associates L.C. from 1993 until 2001. From 1989 to 1993, Armitage served in various high-level diplomatic positions, including as a special emissary to Jordan's King Hussein during the 1991 Gulf War and director of U.S. assistance to the new independent states of the former Soviet Union. Prior to this, Armitage served in the Pentagon as the assistant secretary of defense for international security affairs (1983–89) and deputy assistant secretary of defense for East Asia and Pacific affairs (1981–83). Armitage graduated in 1967 from the U.S. Naval Academy and served three combat tours in Vietnam. He is the recipient of numerous U.S. and foreign military decorations as well as awards for distinguished public service. He was awarded a KBE and became a Knight Commander of the Order of St. Michael and St. George and, as of October 13, 2010, he became an Honorary Companion of the Order of Australia.

Reza Aslan is an internationally acclaimed writer and scholar of religion and a contributing editor at the *Daily Beast*. He is an associate professor of creative writing at the University of California, Riverside, and a senior fellow at the Orfalea Center for Global and International Studies at the University of California, Santa Barbara. He is president and CEO of Aslan Media Inc., a frequent commentator on CNN, CBS, and NPR, and cofounder and creative director of BoomGen Studios. He is a member of the Council on Foreign Relations, the Los Angeles Institute for the Humanities, and the Pacific Council on International Policy. He also serves on the board of directors of the Ploughshares Fund, Abraham's Vision, and PEN USA. Aslan's first book is the international best seller *No god but God: The Origins, Evolution, and Future of Islam*, which has been translated into thirteen languages and was named one of the one hundred most important books of the last decade. Aslan has degrees in religions from Santa Clara University, Harvard University, and the University of California, Santa Barbara, as well as an MFA from the University of Iowa, where he was named the Truman Capote fellow in fiction.

J. Brian Atwood became dean of the Humphrey Institute of Public Affairs in October 2002. He served for six years as administrator of the U.S. Agency for International Development (USAID) during the Clinton administration. In the Clinton administration, Atwood led the transition team at the State Department and was undersecretary of state for management before being appointed head of USAID. During the Carter administration, Atwood served as assistant secretary of state for congressional relations. He was dean of professional studies and academic affairs at the Foreign Service Institute from 1981 to 1982 and the first president of the National Democratic Institute for International Affairs (1986–93). In 2001, Atwood served on UN Secretary General Kofi Annan's panel on peace operations. He writes and speaks frequently on international development, postconflict reconstruction, foreign policy, the role of the United Nations and other multilateral organizations in international affairs, and the U.S. role in the world order. He holds a BA in government and history from Boston University and received an honorary doctorate of laws from American University. He joined the Foreign Service in 1966 and served in the U.S. embassies in Cote d'Ivoire and Spain.

David W. Barno is a senior adviser and senior fellow at the Center for a New American Security. A career Army officer, he retired as a three-star general in 2006 after a thirty-year career. General Barno commanded all U.S. and coalition forces in Afghanistan for nineteen months from 2003 to 2005; his military command responsibilities included Afghanistan, Pakistan, and parts of Central Asia under U.S. Central Command. His military career was highlighted by command at every level in the U.S. Army from lieutenant to lieutenant general, and extensive service in airborne, infantry, and special operations units. Commissioned as an infantry officer from the U.S. Military Academy at West Point in 1976, he also holds an MA in national security studies from Georgetown University and is a graduate of the U.S. Army Command and General Staff College and the U.S. Army War College. Following his retirement from active service, he served for four years as the director of the Near East South Asia Center for Strategic Studies at the National Defense University. From 2007 to 2009, he served as chairman of the Secretary of Veterans Affairs Advisory Committee on Operation Iraqi Freedom and Enduring Freedom Veterans, Families and Survivors.

Samuel R. Berger is chair of Albright Stonebridge Group, a global strategy firm. Berger works across many of the firm's engagements, with a strong focus on Asia, Russia and Central Asia, and the Middle East. He is also a principal of Albright Capital Management LLC. Berger served as national security adviser to President Bill Clinton from 1997 until 2001, as deputy national security adviser during Clinton's first term, as senior foreign policy adviser to Governor Clinton during his 1992 presidential campaign, and as director of national security for the 1992 Clinton-Gore transition. Prior to his service in the Clinton administration, Berger served as special assistant to former New York City mayor John Lindsay and as legislative assistant to former U.S. senator Harold Hughes (D-IA) and former congressman Joseph Resnick (D-NY). Berger also served as deputy director of the State Department's policy planning staff from 1977 to 1980. Currently, Berger is co-chairing a project on the Middle East peace process with the United States Institute of Peace. He is an active participant in the Aspen Institute's U.S.-India Strategic Dialogue and serves on the international advisory council of the Brookings Doha Center. Berger received his BA from Cornell University and his JD from Harvard Law School.

Karan K. Bhatia joined General Electric Co. in 2007 as vice president and senior counsel for international law and policy. At GE, he oversees the company's engagement on public policy issues with governments around the world and works to expand its presence in global markets. In November 2005, Ambassador Bhatia was confirmed by the Senate to serve as deputy U.S. trade representative (USTR), overseeing U.S. trade policy with Asia and Africa. Before joining USTR, he served as assistant secretary for aviation and international affairs at the U.S.

Department of Transportation, where he crafted U.S. international and domestic aviation policy and supervised the negotiation of international air services agreements with more than twenty countries. Prior to that, he served in the Department of Commerce, where he was deputy undersecretary and chief counsel for the Bureau of Industry and Security, the U.S. government agency that administers U.S. export controls. Before joining the Bush administration in 2001, he was an equity partner at the Wilmer, Cutler, and Pickering law firm, where he was a member of the firm's international and corporate groups. He holds a BA from Princeton University, an MA from the London School of Economics, and a JD from Columbia University.

Marshall M. Bouton became president of the Chicago Council on Global Affairs in August 2001. Before that, he served for twenty years at the Asia Society in New York, most recently as executive vice president and chief operating officer. Previous positions include director for policy analysis in the Office of the Deputy Assistant Secretary of Defense for Near East, Africa, and South Asia; special assistant to the U. S. ambassador to India; executive secretary for the Indo-U.S. Subcommission on Education and Culture; and program director for India affairs at the Asia Society. Bouton earned a BA in history at Harvard, an MA in South Asian studies from the University of Pennsylvania, and a PhD in political science at the University of Chicago in 1980.

Steve Coll is president of the New America Foundation and a staff writer at the *New Yorker*. Previously, he spent twenty years as a foreign correspondent and senior editor at the *Washington Post*, serving as managing editor from 1998 to 2004. Coll's professional awards include two Pulitzer Prizes. He won the first of these, for explanatory journalism, in 1990, for his series with David A. Vise about the SEC. His second was awarded in 2005, for his book *Ghost Wars*, which also won the Council on Foreign Relations' Arthur Ross Book Award, the Overseas Press Club Award, and the Lionel Gelber Prize for best book published on international affairs during 2004. Other awards include the 1992 Livingston Award for outstanding foreign reporting, the 2000 Robert F. Kennedy Memorial Award for his coverage of the civil war in Sierra Leone, and a second Overseas Press Club Award for international magazine writing. Coll graduated from Occidental College in 1980 with a BA in English and history.

Joseph J. Collins joined the National War College faculty in 2004 as professor of national security strategy. Before this assignment, Collins served for three years as deputy assistant secretary of defense for stability operations, the Pentagon's senior civilian official for peacekeeping, humanitarian assistance, and stabilization-reconstruction operations in Afghanistan. From 1998 to 2001, he was a senior fellow at the Center for Strategic and International Studies, where he wrote major studies on economic sanctions, military culture, and national security policy. A retired Army colonel, his twenty-eight years of military service were divided equally between infantry and armor assignments in the United States, South Korea, and Germany; a decade teaching at West Point in the Department of Social Sciences; and a decade-long series of policy assignments on the Army and Joint Staffs, and in the Office of the Secretary of Defense. He has been a life member of the Council on Foreign Relations since 1992 and received a doctorate in political science from Columbia University.

James F. Dobbins has held a number of State Department and White House posts, including assistant secretary of state for Europe, special assistant to the president, special adviser to the president and secretary of state for the Balkans, and ambassador to the European community. Dobbins had numerous crisis management and diplomatic troubleshooting assignments as the Clinton administration's and, more recently, the Bush administration's special envoy for Afghanistan, Kosovo, Bosnia, Haiti, and Somalia. Past diplomatic assignments include the withdrawal of American forces from Somalia, the American-led multilateral intervention in Haiti, the stabilization and reconstruction of Bosnia, and the NATO intervention in Kosovo. In the wake of September 11, 2001, he was named the Bush administration's representative to the Afghan opposition with the task of putting together and installing a broadly based successor to the Taliban regime. He represented the United States at the Bonn Conference that established the new Afghan government, and, on December 16, 2001, raised the flag over the newly reopened U.S. embassy.

C. Christine Fair is an assistant professor in the Center for Peace and Security Studies at Georgetown University's Edmund A. Walsh School of Foreign Service. She is also a senior fellow with the Counterterrorism Center at West Point and a research fellow with the National Bureau of Asia Research's National Asia Research Program. Prior to joining Georgetown, she served as a senior political scientist with the RAND Corporation, a political officer to the United Nations Assistance Mission to Afghanistan in Kabul, and a senior research associate with the United States Institute of Peace. Her research focuses on political and military affairs in South Asia. She has authored, coauthored and coedited several books and has written numerous peer-reviewed articles covering a range of security issues in Afghanistan, Bangladesh, India, Pakistan, and Sri Lanka. She is a member of the International Institute of Strategic Studies and the Council on Foreign Relations, serves on the editorial board of *Studies in Conflict and Terrorism* and the *Journal of Strategic Studies*, and is an associate editor of *India Review*. Fair has an MA from the Harris School of Public Policy and a PhD from the Department of South Asian Languages and Civilization, both at the University of Chicago.

John A. Gastright is the vice president for government affairs at Dyn-Corp International. In 2005, he joined the Bureau of South Asian Affairs as a deputy assistant secretary, where he focused primarily on Pakistan, Bangladesh, and Afghanistan. Before this appointment, Gastright was the director of House Affairs, Bureau of Legislative Affairs at the Department of State. His State Department service also included a brief term as the acting coordinator for Afghanistan in 2004. He first joined the Department of State as the special assistant to the deputy secretary of state, Richard L. Armitage, and from 2003 to 2004 he served as the staff specialist for South Asia. Before his service with the Department of State, he served on Capitol Hill as chief of staff to Representative Jack Kingston (R-GA) and as projects director and military assistant to Senator Strom Thurmond (R-SC). He previously served as a naval officer from 1988 to 1994 and as a police officer from 1987 to 1988 with the City of Charleston, South Carolina. Gastright received a BA in political science from the Citadel, an MA in national security studies from the U.S. Naval War College, and an MA in congressional studies from the Catholic University of America.

Robert L. Grenier is chairman of ERG Partners, which provides strategic and financial consulting services for firms in the security industry. He is a highly decorated twenty-seven-year veteran of the Central Intelligence Agency's (CIA) Clandestine Service. A specialist in the Near East and South Asia with fifteen years' experience in foreign postings,

Grenier has most recently served as director of the CIA's Counter-terrorism Center (2004–2006), as the CIA's Iraq mission manager (2002–2004), and as the CIA's chief of station in Islamabad, Pakistan (1999–2002). Earlier in his career, he was deputy national intelligence officer for the Near East and South Asia and a special assistant to the undersecretary of state. He conceived and organized the CIA's Counter-Proliferation Division, serving as its first chief of operations. He was also chief of the CIA's basic training facility, and authored the Clandestine Service's code of ethics. Grenier received an AB in philosophy from Dartmouth College and later did graduate studies at the University of Virginia. He has appeared widely in both broadcast and print media and writes frequently on intelligence and foreign policy topics.

John M. Keane is a senior partner at SCP Partners. A four-star general, he completed thirty-seven years of public service in 2003, culminating as acting chief of staff and vice chief of staff of the U.S. Army. General Keane is a career paratrooper, a combat veteran of Vietnam decorated for valor, who spent much of his military life in operational commands where his units were employed in Somalia, Haiti, Bosnia, and Kosovo. He commanded the 101st Airborne Division (Air Assault) and the 18th Airborne Corps, the Army's largest war fighting organization. He was in the Pentagon on 9/11 and provided oversight and support for the wars in Afghanistan and Iraq. He is a member of the secretary of defense's policy board and played a major role in recommending the "surge strategy" in Iraq. General Keane graduated with a BS in accounting from Fordham University and with an MA in philosophy from Western Kentucky University. He is a graduate of the Army War College and the Command and General Staff College.

Michael Krepon is cofounder of the Henry L. Stimson Center and teaches in the politics department at the University of Virginia. He is the author or editor of thirteen books and more than 350 articles. He divides his time between Stimson's South Asia and space security projects. The South Asia project concentrates on escalation control, nuclear risk reduction, confidence-building, and peacemaking between India and Pakistan. This project entails field work, publications, and Washington-based programming, including a visiting fellowship program. The space security project seeks to promote a code of conduct for responsible space-faring nations and works toward stronger international norms for the peaceful uses of outer space. Before cofounding the Stimson Center, he worked at the Carnegie Endowment for International Peace, the U.S. Arms Control and Disarmament Agency during the Carter administration, and in the U.S. House of Representatives, assisting Congressman Norm Dicks (D-WA). He received a BA from Franklin & Marshall College and an MA from the School of Advanced International Studies, Johns Hopkins University. He also studied Arabic at the American University in Cairo, Egypt.

Sloan C. Mann is the cofounder and managing director of Development Transformations (DT), a small veteran-owned company that focuses on improving the capability, capacity, and effectiveness of civilian and military personnel involved in conflict and postconflict environments. Before founding DT, he held a diverse array of jobs in the military, private, and public sectors. From 2007 to 2009, he was U.S. Agency for International Development (USAID) development adviser to the U.S. Special Forces in Afghanistan. Mann worked for a number of different offices at USAID, including the Office of Foreign Disaster Assistance (OFDA) and the Office of Transition Initiatives (OTI). He was a field program officer with OFDA responsible for all operations in southern and western Darfur, Sudan. In Iraq as a member of the Disaster Assistance Response Team and OTI, he worked one year as an abuse prevention officer focusing on identifying, monitoring, and preventing human rights violations. While in the military, Mann served as a U.S. Army infantry officer from 1997 to 2002 and was a member of peacekeeping deployments to Bosnia-Herzegovina and Kosovo. Mann received a BS in international politics from West Point and an MA from the School of Foreign Service at Georgetown University.

Daniel S. Markey is senior fellow for India, Pakistan and South Asia at the Council on Foreign Relations, where he specializes in security and governance issues in South Asia. From 2003 to 2007, Markey held the South Asia portfolio on the secretary's Policy Planning Staff at the U.S. Department of State. Prior to government service, he taught in the Department of Politics at Princeton University, served as executive director of Princeton's Research Program in International Security, and was a postdoctoral fellow at Harvard's Olin Institute for Strategic Studies. He received a BA in international studies from Johns Hopkins University and a PhD from Princeton's Department of Politics.

John A. Nagl is the president of the Center for a New American Security. He is a visiting professor in the War Studies Department at King's College London and a member of the Defense Policy Board, the Council on Foreign Relations, Veterans of Foreign Wars, and the International Institute of Strategic Studies. He served as an armor officer in the U.S. Army for twenty years, retiring with the rank of lieutenant colonel. He taught national security studies at West Point's Department of Social Sciences and in Georgetown University's security studies program. He served as a military assistant to two deputy secretaries of defense and later worked as a senior fellow at the Center for a New American Security. He was awarded the Combat Action Badge by General James Mattis of the U.S. Marine Corps, under whose leadership he fought in Al Anbar in 2004. Nagl was a distinguished graduate of the U.S. Military Academy and earned an MA in military arts and sciences from the Command and General Staff College, where he received the George C. Marshall Award as the top graduate. He earned his PhD from Oxford University as a Rhodes scholar.

John D. Negroponte joined McLarty Associates as vice chairman in 2009 following a distinguished career in diplomacy and national security. Ambassador Negroponte held government positions abroad and in Washington between 1960 and 1997 and again from 2001 to 2008. He has been ambassador to Honduras, Mexico, the Philippines, the United Nations, and Iraq. In Washington he served twice on the National Security Council staff, first as director for Vietnam in the Nixon administration and then as deputy national security adviser under President Ronald Reagan. He has also held a cabinet-level position as the first director of national intelligence under President George W. Bush. His most recent position in government was as deputy secretary of state, where he served as chief operating officer. While in the private sector, he was executive vice president of the McGraw-Hill Companies and chairman of the French-American Foundation. He recently became a distinguished senior research fellow in grand strategy and a lecturer in international affairs at Yale University. He also serves as chairman of the Council of the Americas/Americas Society and as a trustee of the Asia Society. He has received numerous awards, including the State Department's Distinguished Service Medal on two separate occasions. In 2009 President Bush awarded Ambassador Negroponte the National Security Medal.

Charles S. Robb joined the faculty of George Mason University as a distinguished professor of law and public policy in 2001. Previously, he served as lieutenant governor of Virginia, as Virginia's sixty-fourth governor (1982–86), and as a U.S. senator (1989–2001). While in the Senate, he became the only member to serve simultaneously on all three national security committees (Intelligence, Armed Services, and Foreign Relations). He also served on the Finance, Commerce, and Budget committees. During the 1960s, he served on active duty with the U.S. Marine Corps, retiring from the Marine Corps Reserve in 1991. He received his JD from the University of Virginia in 1973, clerked for Judge John D. Butzner Jr. on the U.S. Court of Appeals for the Fourth Circuit, and practiced law with Williams and Connolly before being elected to state office. He was a partner at Hunton and Williams and a fellow at Harvard University's Institute of Politics and William & Mary's Marshall Wythe School of Law. Since leaving the Senate in 2001, he has served as chairman of numerous organizations, including the Board of Visitors at the U.S. Naval Academy and the President's Commission on Intelligence Capabilities of the United States Regarding Weapons of Mass Destruction.

Teresita C. Schaffer is director of the South Asia Program at the Center for Strategic and International Studies. Her areas of expertise include U.S.-South Asia relations, regional security, and economics, energy, and health policy in India. During her thirty-year career in the U.S. Foreign Service, she specialized in international economics and South Asia, on which she was one of the State Department's principal experts. From 1989 to 1992, she served as deputy assistant secretary of state for South Asia, at that time the senior South Asia position in the department. From 1992 to 1995, she served as U.S. ambassador to Sri Lanka, and from 1995 to 1997, as director of the Foreign Service Institute. Her earlier posts included Tel Aviv, Islamabad, New Delhi, and Dhaka, as well as a tour as director of the Office of International Trade in the State Department. After retiring from the Foreign Service, Schaffer spent a year as a consultant on business issues relating to South Asia. She has also taught at Georgetown University and American University. Schaffer speaks French, Swedish, German, Italian, Hebrew, Hindi, and Urdu and has studied Bangla and Sinhala.

Shirin R. Tahir-Kheli is currently a scholar at the Carnegie Corporation of New York and is working on a monograph, "Diplomacy Without Negotiation: America's Outreach to the Muslim World 2003–2006." Recently, Ambassador Tahir-Kheli was Secretary of State Condoleezza Rice's senior adviser for women's empowerment. Before this, she served as the secretary's senior adviser on United Nations reform. From 2003 to 2005, she was the special assistant to the president and senior director for democracy, human rights, and international operations at the National Security Council. From 1993 to 1995, she was a senior fellow at the Center of International Studies at Princeton University. From 1984 to 1990, she served as director for South Asian Affairs on the National Security Council. From 1982 to 1984, she was a member of the Policy Planning Staff at the Department of State. The author of numerous books and articles on U.S.-Pakistan relations, Ambassador Tahir-Kheli has been a member of the Council on Foreign Relations since 1990. She has a BA from Ohio Wesleyan University and an MA and a PhD in international relations from the University of Pennsylvania.

Ashley J. Tellis is a senior associate at the Carnegie Endowment for International Peace specializing in international security, defense, and Asian strategic issues. While on assignment to the U.S. Department of State as senior adviser to the undersecretary of state for political affairs, he was intimately involved in negotiating the civil nuclear agreement with India. Previously, Tellis was commissioned into the Foreign Service and served as senior adviser to the ambassador at the U.S. embassy in New Delhi. He also served on the National Security Council staff as special assistant to the president and senior director for Strategic Planning and Southwest Asia. Before his government service, he was senior policy analyst at the RAND Corporation and professor of policy analysis at the RAND graduate school. He is the research director of the Strategic Asia program at the National Bureau of Asian Research. He is also a member of the Council on Foreign Relations, the International Institute of Strategic Studies, the U.S. Naval Institute, and the Navy League of the United States. Tellis received a BA and an MA from the University of Bombay and an MA and a PhD from the University of Chicago.

John W. Warner is a senior adviser at Hogan Lovells. He rejoined the firm after deciding not to seek a sixth term as U.S. senator for the

Commonwealth of Virginia. During his thirty years in the Senate, he served on the Senate Armed Services Committee. He also served on the Senate Health, Education, and Pensions Committee; Committee on Homeland Security and Governmental Affairs; Select Committee on Intelligence; Commerce Committee; Environment and Public Works Committee; and Rules Committee. Senator Warner volunteered for two periods of active military duty, the first as an enlisted sailor in the final years of World War II and the second as a lieutenant in the U.S. Marines during the Korean War. Between 1953 and 1960, he clerked for the Honorable E. Barrett Prettyman, U.S. Court of Appeals for the District of Columbia Circuit, and was an assistant U.S. attorney for the District of Columbia. He joined Hogan & Hartson as an associate in 1961 and became a partner in 1964. In 1969, he was appointed and confirmed by the Senate as undersecretary, and later as secretary, of the U.S. Navy. Senator Warner received a BS from Washington and Lee University and an LLB from the University of Virginia School of Law.

Andrew Wilder is the director of Afghanistan and Pakistan programs at the United States Institute of Peace (USIP). Prior to joining USIP, he was a research director at Tufts University's Feinstein International Center. Previously, he worked in Afghanistan, where he established and was the director of Afghanistan's first independent policy research institution, the Afghanistan Research and Evaluation Unit. Between 1986 and 2001, he worked for several international NGOs managing humanitarian and development programs in Pakistan and Afghanistan. He served as the director of the Pakistan/Afghanistan program of Save the Children (U.S.) for six years. He is the author of *The Pakistani Voter* and a coauthor of *A Guide to Government in Afghanistan*. His recent research and publications have looked at the effectiveness of aid in promoting stabilization objectives in Afghanistan, police reform policies in Afghanistan, Afghan refugee education policy in Pakistan, the politics of civil service reform in Pakistan, electoral politics and policies in Pakistan and Afghanistan, and the politics of subnational administration in Afghanistan. Wilder has a BSFS degree from Georgetown University and an MALD and a PhD from the Fletcher School of Law and Diplomacy at Tufts University.

Task Force Observers

Wendy R. Anderson is special assistant to Dr. Ashton Carter, undersecretary of defense for acquisition, technology, and logistics, at the U.S. Department of Defense. Most recently, she served as professional staff on the U.S. Senate Homeland Security and Governmental Affairs Committee, managing the international security portfolio for the Subcommittee on Federal Financial Management, Government Information, Federal Services, and International Security, and was lead staff on South Asia and the Middle East. During the 2008 presidential campaign, she was a member of Senator Obama's South Asia policy team. During her Senate tenure, she also served as the intelligence liaison for Senator Barbara Mikulski (D-MD) and as defense adviser for Senator Frank Lautenberg (D-NJ). As deputy director for external affairs in the Women and Public Policy Program at Harvard's Kennedy School of Government, Anderson worked on postconflict reconstruction in South Asia and the Middle East. Earlier, as a Thomas J. Watson Fellowship recipient, she studied the prevention of deadly conflict in those same regions. Anderson received a BA from Hendrix College, an MA in religion from Harvard University, and an MA in international affairs from Columbia University. She is a term member of the Council on Foreign Relations.

Stephen D. Biddle is the Roger Hertog senior fellow for defense policy at the Council on Foreign Relations (CFR). Previously, he held the Elihu Root chair in military studies at the U.S. Army War College Strategic Studies Institute. A member of the Defense Policy Board, Biddle served on General Stanley McChrystal's Initial Strategic Assessment Team in 2009, on General David Petraeus's Joint Strategic Assessment Team in 2007, and as a senior adviser to General Petraeus's Central Command Assessment Team in 2008–2009. He is codirector of the Columbia University Summer Workshop on the Analysis of Military

Operations and Strategy and holds an appointment as adjunct associate professor of international and public affairs at Columbia University. His book *Military Power: Explaining Victory and Defeat in Modern Battle* has won four prizes, including CFR's Arthur Ross Book Award Silver Medal and the 2005 Huntington Prize from the Harvard University Olin Institute for Strategic Studies. He was awarded the U.S. Army Superior Civilian Service Medal in 2003 and 2006 and in 2007 was presented with the U.S. Army Commander's Award for Public Service in Baghdad. Biddle received an AB, an MPP, and a PhD in public policy from Harvard University.

Jonah Blank is policy director for South and Southeast Asia on the majority staff of the Senate Foreign Relations Committee. Before entering government service in 1999, Blank served as senior editor and foreign correspondent for *U.S. News & World Report*. He has taught anthropology and politics at Harvard and Georgetown and currently teaches at the Johns Hopkins University School of Advanced International Studies. An anthropologist by training, he is author of *Mullahs on the Mainframe: Islam and Modernity Among the Daudi Bohras* and *Arrow of the Blue-Skinned God: Retracing the Ramayana Through India*. He earned his BA in history from Yale and his PhD in anthropology from Harvard.

Kara L. Bue is a partner at Armitage International, L.C., an international business consulting firm. From 2003 to 2005, Bue served as deputy assistant secretary of state for regional stability within the Bureau of Political-Military Affairs (PM). Her direct responsibilities included supervision of the Offices of Regional Security and Arms Transfers; Plans, Policy and Analysis; and Weapons Removal and Abatement. Prior to her position within PM, she served for nearly two years as special assistant to Deputy Secretary of State Richard L. Armitage. Bue advised the deputy secretary on South Asia, international security, and counterterrorism matters. Prior to government service, Bue was in private practice as a corporate and securities lawyer, specializing in financial services law. In addition, she has held positions with the Office of the Secretary of Defense, Department of the Army, and the Federal Bureau of Investigation. Bue is a graduate of Brown University and Loyola Law School, Los Angeles. She is admitted to practice law in California and the District of Columbia.

Isobel Coleman is senior fellow for U.S. foreign policy at the Council on Foreign Relations, where she directs the Civil Society, Markets, and Democracy initiative and the Women and Foreign Policy program. Her areas of expertise include democratization, civil society, economic development, regional gender issues, educational reform, and microfinance. She is the author and coauthor of numerous publications, including most recently *Paradise Beneath Her Feet: How Women are Transforming the Middle East*. In 2010, she served as a track leader for the Clinton Global Initiative. Before joining the Council on Foreign Relations, Coleman was CEO of a healthcare services company and a partner with McKinsey & Company in New York. A Marshall scholar, she holds a BA in public policy and East Asian studies from Princeton University and an MPhil and DPhil in international relations from Oxford University. She serves on several nonprofit boards, including those of Plan USA and Student Sponsor Partners.

Zachary S. Davis is senior fellow at the Center for Global Security Research and an analyst with Z Division, both at Lawrence Livermore National Laboratory, where he specializes in South Asia. Davis was an analyst at the Congressional Research Service, where he worked with Congress members and staff to develop nonproliferation, arms control, export control, and sanctions legislation. He has served in the State Department, the Arms Control and Disarmament Agency, the National Counterproliferation Center, and the White House. Davis is a visiting research professor at the Naval Postgraduate School, where he teaches courses on counterproliferation. He received a BA from the University of California, Santa Cruz, and an MA and a PhD from the University of Virginia. His latest publication is a forthcoming edited volume, *The India-Pakistan Military Standoff: The 2002 Twin Peaks Crisis and Beyond*.

Bjarne M. Iverson serves as the chief of staff, 25th Infantry Division, Schofield Barracks, Hawaii. He will deploy with the division to Iraq in December 2010 for a one-year assignment. He joined the Tropic Lightning Division after completing a one-year assignment as the U.S. Army's military fellow at the Council on Foreign Relations. Most recently, Colonel Iverson served a seventeen-month assignment as the executive officer to General David H. Petraeus in Iraq and at U.S. Central Command. Colonel Iverson received his commission as an engineer officer and concurrently serves as a Middle East foreign area officer. He has been assigned to a variety of command and staff assignments throughout the United States, Latin America, Europe, and the Middle East, including participation in operations Just Cause, Desert Shield, Desert Storm, Desert Fox, Desert Thunder, and Iraqi Freedom (three tours). Colonel Iverson holds a BS from George Mason University, an MA from Princeton University, an MS from the U.S. Army War College, and a certification from the Defense Language Institute for Arabic.

Meghan L. O'Sullivan is an adjunct senior fellow at the Council on Foreign Relations and the Evron and Jeane Kirkpatrick professor of the practice of international affairs at the Harvard Kennedy School. From July 2004 to September 2007, she was special assistant to President George W. Bush and also held the position of deputy national security adviser for Iraq and Afghanistan for the last two years of this tenure. In that role, O'Sullivan led a team of military and diplomatic personnel, lawyers, economists, and political appointees in the Iraq and Afghan directorates at the National Security Council. O'Sullivan also held the positions of senior director for strategic planning and Southwest Asia at the NSC; political adviser to the Coalition Provisional Authority administrator and deputy director for governance in Baghdad; chief adviser to the presidential envoy to the Northern Ireland peace process; and fellow at the Brookings Institution. She has been awarded the Defense Department's highest honor for civilians, the Distinguished Public Service Medal, and three times was awarded the State Department's Superior Honor Award. O'Sullivan holds a BA from Georgetown University and an MSc in economics and a DPhil in politics from Oxford University.

Marisa L. Porges was an international affairs fellow at the Council on Foreign Relations from 2009 to 2010. Her areas of specialization are counterterrorism strategies, including efforts to counter radicalization and combat terrorist financing; detention operations; and Yemen. Her most recent research compared global efforts to deradicalize terrorists after capture and incorporated fieldwork in Afghanistan, Indonesia, Saudi Arabia, Singapore, and Yemen. Prior to joining CFR, Porges was a counterterrorism policy adviser at the U.S. Department of the Treasury and a member of General Petraeus's Central Command Assessment Team. She also served in the Office of the Secretary of Defense for Policy, as an adviser with the Office of Detainee Affairs.

Her responsibilities included negotiating with foreign governments and coordinating U.S. government efforts to repatriate detainees from Guantanamo Bay, Cuba, and Afghanistan. Porges is a commissioned naval flight officer, serving on active duty flying the Navy's EA-6B Prowler and deploying aboard the USS *Lincoln* during Operation Unified Assistance. She received an AB in geophysics from Harvard University and an MSc in government from the London School of Economics. She is currently pursuing a PhD in war studies at King's College London.

Daniel Silverberg serves as deputy counsel on the staff of the U.S. House of Representatives. In this capacity, he provides strategic and procedural counsel to members on legislation moving through committee and on the House floor. Silverberg's legislative portfolio includes defense issues. Previously, he served as an attorney in the Office of General Counsel in the U.S. Department of Defense, with responsibilities related to the Special Operations and Low Intensity Conflict directorate. Before that, he practiced law with Orrick, Herrington & Sutcliffe LLP in San Francisco, where he focused on commercial litigation and white-collar criminal defense matters. Silverberg holds an AB in comparative study of religion from Harvard College and a JD from Stanford Law School.

Independent Task Force Reports

Published by the Council on Foreign Relations

U.S. Policy Toward the Korean Peninsula
Charles L. Pritchard and John H. Tilelli Jr., Chairs; Scott A. Snyder, Project Director
Independent Task Force Report No. 64 (2010)

U.S. Immigration Policy
Jeb Bush and Thomas F. McLarty III, Chairs; Edward Alden, Project Director
Independent Task Force Report No. 63 (2009)

U.S. Nuclear Weapons Policy
William J. Perry and Brent Scowcroft, Chairs; Charles D. Ferguson, Project Director
Independent Task Force Report No. 62 (2009)

Confronting Climate Change: A Strategy for U.S. Foreign Policy
George E. Pataki and Thomas J. Vilsack, Chairs; Michael A. Levi, Project Director
Independent Task Force Report No. 61 (2008)

U.S.-Latin America Relations: A New Direction for a New Reality
Charlene Barshefsky and James T. Hill, Chairs; Shannon O'Neil, Project Director
Independent Task Force Report No. 60 (2008)

U.S.-China Relations: An Affirmative Agenda, A Responsible Course
Carla A. Hills and Dennis C. Blair, Chairs; Frank Sampson Jannuzi, Project Director
Independent Task Force Report No. 59 (2007)

National Security Consequences of U.S. Oil Dependency
John Deutch and James R. Schlesinger, Chairs; David G. Victor, Project Director
Independent Task Force Report No. 58 (2006)

Russia's Wrong Direction: What the United States Can and Should Do
John Edwards and Jack Kemp, Chairs; Stephen Sestanovich, Project Director
Independent Task Force Report No. 57 (2006)

More than Humanitarianism: A Strategic U.S. Approach Toward Africa
Anthony Lake and Christine Todd Whitman, Chairs; Princeton N. Lyman and J. Stephen Morrison, Project Directors
Independent Task Force Report No. 56 (2006)

In the Wake of War: Improving Post-Conflict Capabilities
Samuel R. Berger and Brent Scowcroft, Chairs; William L. Nash, Project Director; Mona K. Sutphen, Deputy Director
Independent Task Force Report No. 55 (2005)

In Support of Arab Democracy: Why and How
Madeleine K. Albright and Vin Weber, Chairs; Steven A. Cook, Project Director
Independent Task Force Report No. 54 (2005)

Building a North American Community
John P. Manley, Pedro Aspe, and William F. Weld, Chairs; Thomas d'Aquino, Andrés
Rozental, and Robert Pastor, Vice Chairs; Chappell H. Lawson, Project Director
Independent Task Force Report No. 53 (2005)

Iran: Time for a New Approach
Zbigniew Brzezinski and Robert M. Gates, Chairs; Suzanne Maloney, Project Director
Independent Task Force Report No. 52 (2004)

An Update on the Global Campaign Against Terrorist Financing
Maurice R. Greenberg, Chair; William F. Wechsler and Lee S. Wolosky, Project Directors
Independent Task Force Report No. 40B (Web-only release, 2004)

Renewing the Atlantic Partnership
Henry A. Kissinger and Lawrence H. Summers, Chairs; Charles A. Kupchan, Project Director
Independent Task Force Report No. 51 (2004)

Iraq: One Year After
Thomas R. Pickering and James R. Schlesinger, Chairs; Eric P. Schwartz, Project Consultant
Independent Task Force Report No. 43C (Web-only release, 2004)

Nonlethal Weapons and Capabilities
Paul X. Kelley and Graham Allison, Chairs; Richard L. Garwin, Project Director
Independent Task Force Report No. 50 (2004)

*New Priorities in South Asia: U.S. Policy Toward India, Pakistan, and Afghanistan
(Chairmen's Report)*
Marshall Bouton, Nicholas Platt, and Frank G. Wisner, Chairs; Dennis Kux and Mahnaz
Ispahani, Project Directors
Independent Task Force Report No. 49 (2003)
Cosponsored with the Asia Society

Finding America's Voice: A Strategy for Reinvigorating U.S. Public Diplomacy
Peter G. Peterson, Chair; Kathy Bloomgarden, Henry Grunwald, David E. Morey, and
Shibley Telhami, Working Committee Chairs; Jennifer Sieg, Project Director; Sharon
Herbstman, Project Coordinator
Independent Task Force Report No. 48 (2003)

Emergency Responders: Drastically Underfunded, Dangerously Unprepared
Warren B. Rudman, Chair; Richard A. Clarke, Senior Adviser; Jamie F. Metzl, Project
Director
Independent Task Force Report No. 47 (2003)

Iraq: The Day After (Chairs' Update)
Thomas R. Pickering and James R. Schlesinger, Chairs; Eric P. Schwartz, Project Director
Independent Task Force Report No. 43B (Web-only release, 2003)

Burma: Time for Change
Mathea Falco, Chair
Independent Task Force Report No. 46 (2003)

Afghanistan: Are We Losing the Peace?
Marshall Bouton, Nicholas Platt, and Frank G. Wisner, Chairs; Dennis Kux and Mahnaz
Ispahani, Project Directors
Chairman's Report of an Independent Task Force (2003)
Cosponsored with the Asia Society

Meeting the North Korean Nuclear Challenge
Morton I. Abramowitz and James T. Laney, Chairs; Eric Heginbotham, Project Director
Independent Task Force Report No. 45 (2003)

Chinese Military Power
Harold Brown, Chair; Joseph W. Prueher, Vice Chair; Adam Segal, Project Director
Independent Task Force Report No. 44 (2003)

Iraq: The Day After
Thomas R. Pickering and James R. Schlesinger, Chairs; Eric P. Schwartz, Project Director
Independent Task Force Report No. 43 (2003)

Threats to Democracy: Prevention and Response
Madeleine K. Albright and Bronislaw Geremek, Chairs; Morton H. Halperin, Director;
Elizabeth Frawley Bagley, Associate Director
Independent Task Force Report No. 42 (2002)

America—Still Unprepared, Still in Danger
Gary Hart and Warren B. Rudman, Chairs; Stephen E. Flynn, Project Director
Independent Task Force Report No. 41 (2002)

Terrorist Financing
Maurice R. Greenberg, Chair; William F. Wechsler and Lee S. Wolosky, Project Directors
Independent Task Force Report No. 40 (2002)

Enhancing U.S. Leadership at the United Nations
David Dreier and Lee H. Hamilton, Chairs; Lee Feinstein and Adrian Karatnycky, Project
Directors
Independent Task Force Report No. 39 (2002)
Cosponsored with Freedom House

Improving the U.S. Public Diplomacy Campaign in the War Against Terrorism
Carla A. Hills and Richard C. Holbrooke, Chairs; Charles G. Boyd, Project Director
Independent Task Force Report No. 38 (Web-only release, 2001)

Building Support for More Open Trade
Kenneth M. Duberstein and Robert E. Rubin, Chairs; Timothy F. Geithner, Project Direc-
tor; Daniel R. Lucich, Deputy Project Director
Independent Task Force Report No. 37 (2001)

Beginning the Journey: China, the United States, and the WTO
Robert D. Hormats, Chair; Elizabeth Economy and Kevin Nealer, Project Directors
Independent Task Force Report No. 36 (2001)

Strategic Energy Policy Update
Edward L. Morse, Chair; Amy Myers Jaffe, Project Director
Independent Task Force Report No. 33B (2001)
Cosponsored with the James A. Baker III Institute for Public Policy of Rice University

Testing North Korea: The Next Stage in U.S. and ROK Policy
Morton I. Abramowitz and James T. Laney, Chairs; Robert A. Manning, Project Director
Independent Task Force Report No. 35 (2001)

The United States and Southeast Asia: A Policy Agenda for the New Administration
J. Robert Kerrey, Chair; Robert A. Manning, Project Director
Independent Task Force Report No. 34 (2001)

Strategic Energy Policy: Challenges for the 21st Century
Edward L. Morse, Chair; Amy Myers Jaffe, Project Director
Independent Task Force Report No. 33 (2001)
Cosponsored with the James A. Baker III Institute for Public Policy of Rice University

A Letter to the President and a Memorandum on U.S. Policy Toward Brazil
Stephen Robert, Chair; Kenneth Maxwell, Project Director
Independent Task Force Report No. 32 (2001)

State Department Reform
Frank C. Carlucci, Chair; Ian J. Brzezinski, Project Coordinator
Independent Task Force Report No. 31 (2001)
Cosponsored with the Center for Strategic and International Studies

U.S.-Cuban Relations in the 21st Century: A Follow-on Report
Bernard W. Aronson and William D. Rogers, Chairs; Julia Sweig and Walter Mead, Project
Directors
Independent Task Force Report No. 30 (2000)

Toward Greater Peace and Security in Colombia: Forging a Constructive U.S. Policy
Bob Graham and Brent Scowcroft, Chairs; Michael Shifter, Project Director
Independent Task Force Report No. 29 (2000)
Cosponsored with the Inter-American Dialogue

Future Directions for U.S. Economic Policy Toward Japan
Laura D'Andrea Tyson, Chair; M. Diana Helweg Newton, Project Director
Independent Task Force Report No. 28 (2000)

First Steps Toward a Constructive U.S. Policy in Colombia
Bob Graham and Brent Scowcroft, Chairs; Michael Shifter, Project Director
Interim Report (2000)
Cosponsored with the Inter-American Dialogue

Promoting Sustainable Economies in the Balkans
Steven Rattner, Chair; Michael B.G. Froman, Project Director
Independent Task Force Report No. 27 (2000)

Non-Lethal Technologies: Progress and Prospects
Richard L. Garwin, Chair; W. Montague Winfield, Project Director
Independent Task Force Report No. 26 (1999)

Safeguarding Prosperity in a Global Financial System:
The Future International Financial Architecture
Carla A. Hills and Peter G. Peterson, Chairs; Morris Goldstein, Project Director
Independent Task Force Report No. 25 (1999)
Cosponsored with the International Institute for Economics

U.S. Policy Toward North Korea: Next Steps
Morton I. Abramowitz and James T. Laney, Chairs; Michael J. Green, Project Director
Independent Task Force Report No. 24 (1999)

Reconstructing the Balkans
Morton I. Abramowitz and Albert Fishlow, Chairs; Charles A. Kupchan, Project Director
Independent Task Force Report No. 23 (Web-only release, 1999)

Strengthening Palestinian Public Institutions
Michel Rocard, Chair; Henry Siegman, Project Director; Yezid Sayigh and Khalil Shikaki,
Principal Authors
Independent Task Force Report No. 22 (1999)

U.S. Policy Toward Northeastern Europe
Zbigniew Brzezinski, Chair; F. Stephen Larrabee, Project Director
Independent Task Force Report No. 21 (1999)

The Future of Transatlantic Relations
Robert D. Blackwill, Chair and Project Director
Independent Task Force Report No. 20 (1999)

U.S.-Cuban Relations in the 21st Century
Bernard W. Aronson and William D. Rogers, Chairs; Walter Russell Mead, Project Director
Independent Task Force Report No. 19 (1999)

After the Tests: U.S. Policy Toward India and Pakistan
Richard N. Haass and Morton H. Halperin, Chairs
Independent Task Force Report No. 18 (1998)
Cosponsored with the Brookings Institution

Managing Change on the Korean Peninsula
Morton I. Abramowitz and James T. Laney, Chairs; Michael J. Green, Project Director
Independent Task Force Report No. 17 (1998)

Promoting U.S. Economic Relations with Africa
Peggy Dulany and Frank Savage, Chairs; Salih Booker, Project Director
Independent Task Force Report No. 16 (1998)

U.S. Middle East Policy and the Peace Process
Henry Siegman, Project Coordinator
Independent Task Force Report No. 15 (1997)

Differentiated Containment: U.S. Policy Toward Iran and Iraq
Zbigniew Brzezinski and Brent Scowcroft, Chairs; Richard W. Murphy, Project Director
Independent Task Force Report No. 14 (1997)

Russia, Its Neighbors, and an Enlarging NATO
Richard G. Lugar, Chair; Victoria Nuland, Project Director
Independent Task Force Report No. 13 (1997)

Rethinking International Drug Control: New Directions for U.S. Policy
Mathea Falco, Chair
Independent Task Force Report No. 12 (1997)

Financing America's Leadership: Protecting American Interests and Promoting American Values
Mickey Edwards and Stephen J. Solarz, Chairs; Morton H. Halperin, Lawrence J. Korb,
and Richard M. Moose, Project Directors
Independent Task Force Report No. 11 (1997)
Cosponsored with the Brookings Institution

A New U.S. Policy Toward India and Pakistan
Richard N. Haass, Chair; Gideon Rose, Project Director
Independent Task Force Report No. 10 (1997)

Arms Control and the U.S.-Russian Relationship
Robert D. Blackwill, Chair and Author; Keith W. Dayton, Project Director
Independent Task Force Report No. 9 (1996)
Cosponsored with the Nixon Center for Peace and Freedom

American National Interest and the United Nations
George Soros, Chair
Independent Task Force Report No. 8 (1996)

Making Intelligence Smarter: The Future of U.S. Intelligence
Maurice R. Greenberg, Chair; Richard N. Haass, Project Director
Independent Task Force Report No. 7 (1996)

Lessons of the Mexican Peso Crisis
John C. Whitehead, Chair; Marie-Josée Kravis, Project Director
Independent Task Force Report No. 6 (1996)

Managing the Taiwan Issue: Key Is Better U.S. Relations with China
Stephen Friedman, Chair; Elizabeth Economy, Project Director
Independent Task Force Report No. 5 (1995)

Non-Lethal Technologies: Military Options and Implications
Malcolm H. Wiener, Chair
Independent Task Force Report No. 4 (1995)

Should NATO Expand?
Harold Brown, Chair; Charles A. Kupchan, Project Director
Independent Task Force Report No. 3 (1995)

Success or Sellout? The U.S.-North Korean Nuclear Accord
Kyung Won Kim and Nicholas Platt, Chairs; Richard N. Haass, Project Director
Independent Task Force Report No. 2 (1995)
Cosponsored with the Seoul Forum for International Affairs

Nuclear Proliferation: Confronting the New Challenges
Stephen J. Hadley, Chair; Mitchell B. Reiss, Project Director
Independent Task Force Report No. 1 (1995)

To purchase a printed copy, call the Brookings Institution Press: 800.537.5487.
Note: Task Force reports are available for download from CFR's website, www.cfr.org.
For more information, email publications@cfr.org.